Making Your own hats

Vol.4

Creative cut-and-join Hat sewing patterns

Size S/M/L/XL for adults
and S/M/L for children

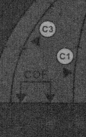

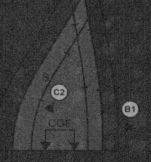

Table of contents

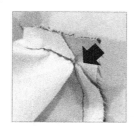

Please read these notes

- All actual-scale patterns and templates are printed on the odd-numbered pages only, with 1-cm square grid background.

- Seam allowance (SA) is **not** included in all patterns yet.

- Due to the limited space, some panels require two pages to display the full patterns.

- Sizing guide:

  Head circumference for adult women;

  size S ~ 55 cm (21 ½ inch)
  size M ~ 57 cm (22 ½ inch)
  size L ~ 59 cm (23 ¼ inch)
  size XL ~ 61.5 cm (24 ¼ inch)

  Head circumference for children;

  size S ~ 48 cm (19 inch)
  size M ~ 50 cm (19 ¾ inch)
  size L ~ 52 cm (20 ½ inch)

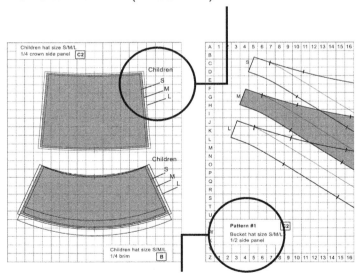 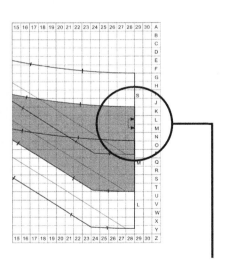

½ pattern means only a half of the relevant pattern is shown (hence two pieces will be needed for the full pattern), and is sometimes used together with the **COF** symbol

COF or **cut-on-fold** symbol; i.e., when the fabric is fold along the grain line, these arrows determine the fold

4

What size fits me?

It is recommended that the head circumference measurement is taken, to help you decide on the size. To measure, just pass a measuring tape around the fullest part of your head, plus popping a tip of your little finger under it to allow some extra space for lining and sweatband.

Depending on the fabrics, thread types, tension, or even the cutting and/or sewing techniques, you may feel your finished sewn hat is somehow bigger or smaller than the actual pattern size. Especially, for six-panel crowns, only about 2.5-3 mm difference in base width per one panel could change the hat to another size already (as any two adjacent sizes have about 2-cm difference in total head circumference length). So, it would be nice to re-check if any correction is needed once the crown is made, just before the final assembly.

You may also consider a one-step bigger size, in case the fabrics and/or sweatband are quite thick. If you are unsure, it may be good to try using some left-over fabrics with similar thickness and/or texture.

Some thoughts about grain line

As all fabrics have stretch on the bias, one should be careful when planning for pattern layout over the fabric. Where you want the pressure to hold, the straight of the grain is preferred. While where a little stretch is beneficial for comfort, some bias can be helpful.

Although this doesn't make a serious issue in hat sewing, and it's a nice idea to utilize your left-overs for these creative hats, each of its crown panel can have a width span 1/3 to 2/3 of the circumference length projection of the hemispheric crown. In such case, no matter how we want to minimize bias stretch, it's unlikely to avoid. As a result of bias pull, rippling wrinkles can happen. This could be especially bold when the fabric is thin.

What we want to suggest is, please try not to use too thin fabrics, or consider adding a fusible interface material under each crown panel, which will also make your sewing easier and more neat. Recommended options for grain line placement, in order to balance bias effect around the entire crown, are also given below. The images show all panels needed for making each crown arranged flat in a cyclic order, with arrows indicating the grain line.

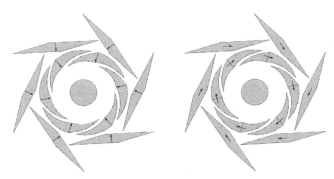

All panels needed for the circuit crown design,
with two recommended grain line options.

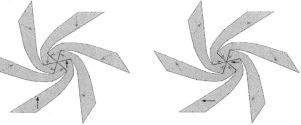

All panels needed for the spiral crown design,
with two recommended grain line options.

Sewing a corner

In one of our creative hat in this volume, you will have a chance to practice skills in corner seam sewing. The first thing you have to do, in order to align the seam to sew, is to clip the seam at and almost up to the point of corner, as well as other points along the curved seams *(a)*.

Then, just start from somewhere above the corner. You may repeat previous stitches a bit *(b)*. Slowly sew as you approach the corner, and stop right at the corner with the needle down in the fabric *(c)*. Lift the presser foot up and pivot the fabric to face the new direction *(d)*. After that, put the foot down and start sewing normally again *(e)*. Then, just check your corner *(f and g)*.

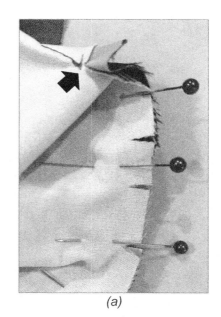

(a)

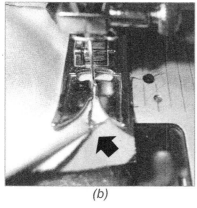

(b)

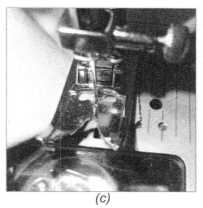

(c)

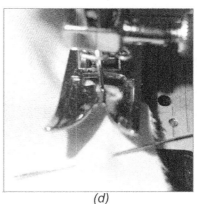

(d)

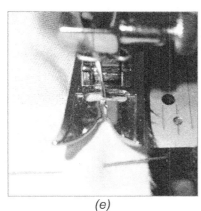

(e)

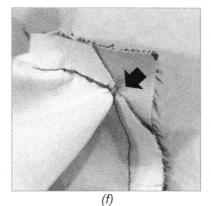

(f)

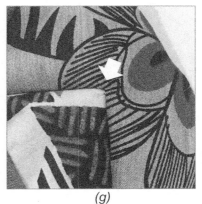

(g)

5-panel star hat, design #1

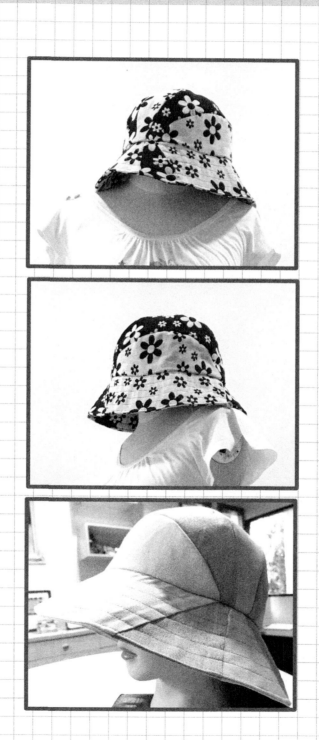

Spiral hat

Creative star hat patterns #1 and #2

- Provided are patterns size S/M/L/XL for adults, and S/M/L for children.

- As multiple sizes are displayed on the same pages, only size M is gray shaded, in order to ease the reading.

- The 5-panel star hat comes with two design options. **Design #1** has multiple seams accumulating at one point, and is only good when the fabric is not too thick. **Design #2** is more practical with some spacing between each seam. For both designs, you have to trim off seam allowances or grade the seams at each accumulating point, on the crown, lining, brim and underbrim, to make it possible and/or more neat to assemble.

- For the crown and lining, **C1** to **C3** shall be used. A total of 5 panels will be needed to make one.

- For the brim and underbrim, **B1** to **B3** shall be used. A total of 8 panels will be needed to make one.

- The actual-size patterns for **C1** to **C3**, and **B1** will be provided in half.

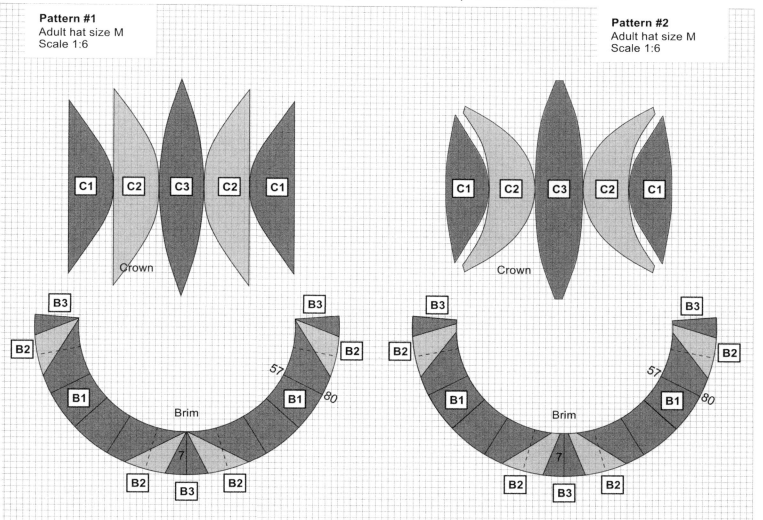

Materials

- Fabric #1 for the crown (**C1**, **C3**), brim (**B1**, **B3**), and underbrim (**B1**, **B3**)

- Fabric #2 for the crown (**C2**), brim (**B2**), and underbrim (**B2**)

- Fabric #3 for lining (**C1, C2, C3**)

- Depending on the fabrics used, making one hat will generally require less than a yard of fabric.

- A sweatband with length equal to your head circumference, plus seam allowance (SA), that circles completely inside the crown at its base will be also needed. You may choose from some leftovers to create one on your own (i.e., a non-bias strip for 2-3 cm wide binding).

- Interface (i.e., iron-on stabilizer), to insert inside the brim, is optional. You don't need any if the fabrics are thick and stiff enough. To prepare the interface, use the same brim template <u>with</u> SA.

- Also, if desired, wadding can be added, to create another soft fluffy layer to be sandwiched between the outer fabrics, and probably with extra texture by stitching multiple rows around. To prepare wadding, use the same brim template <u>with</u> SA.

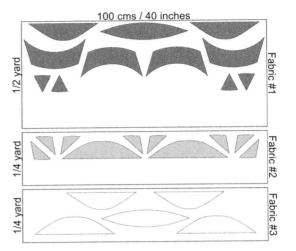

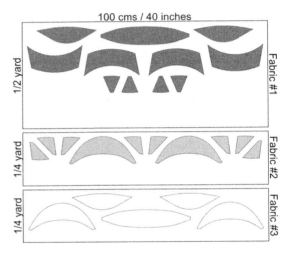

Construction

- **The crown** – Put the right sides of **C1** and **C2** together, and match the seams to sew. You shall clip along SA to relax tension and ease the alignment of the curved seams. Then, repeat the same to join **C3**, **C2**, and **C1**. After that, trim off SA, or grade the seam, to smooth the thickness near seam accumulating points (beware not to snip the thread). Do the same for lining. Then put their wrong sides together, match the bottom seams and stitch on the right side below the intended circumference line to lock the crown and lining together. You may allow 1 cm displacement between them, to smooth further the reduced thickness.

- **The brim** – Stick the interface to each brim panel. Put the right sides of any panel pair together, and match the seams to sew. Then, repeat the same to join the rest in the right order to form a loop. After that, grade the seam, to smooth the thickness near seam accumulating points (beware not to snip the thread). Do the same for the underbrim. Then put their right sides together, and match the outer seams to sew. Trim off and/or clip along SA, turn the right sides out, and make single or double edge stitching. If you'd like to stitch multiple rows around, just do it now.

- **Assembly** – Put the right sides of the crown and brim components together and match the crown-brim seams. Additional clipping along SA would be needed to relax tension and ease the alignment (especially on the concave seam of the brim), before sewing them together. Then you may (or may not) do overlock stitching for tidiness reason. Finally, align the sweatband to the combined seam and stitch over to complete your star hat.

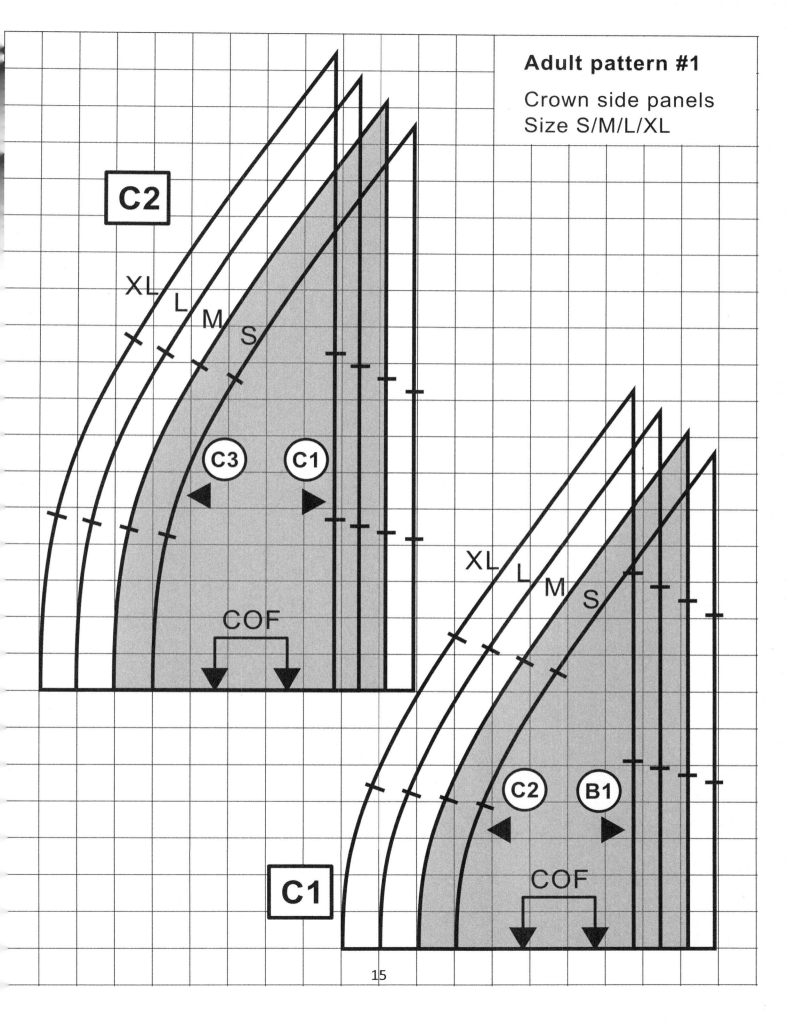

Adult pattern #1

Crown side panels
Size S/M/L/XL

C2

XL L M S

C3 C1

COF

C1

XL L M S

C2 B1

COF

This page is intentionally blank

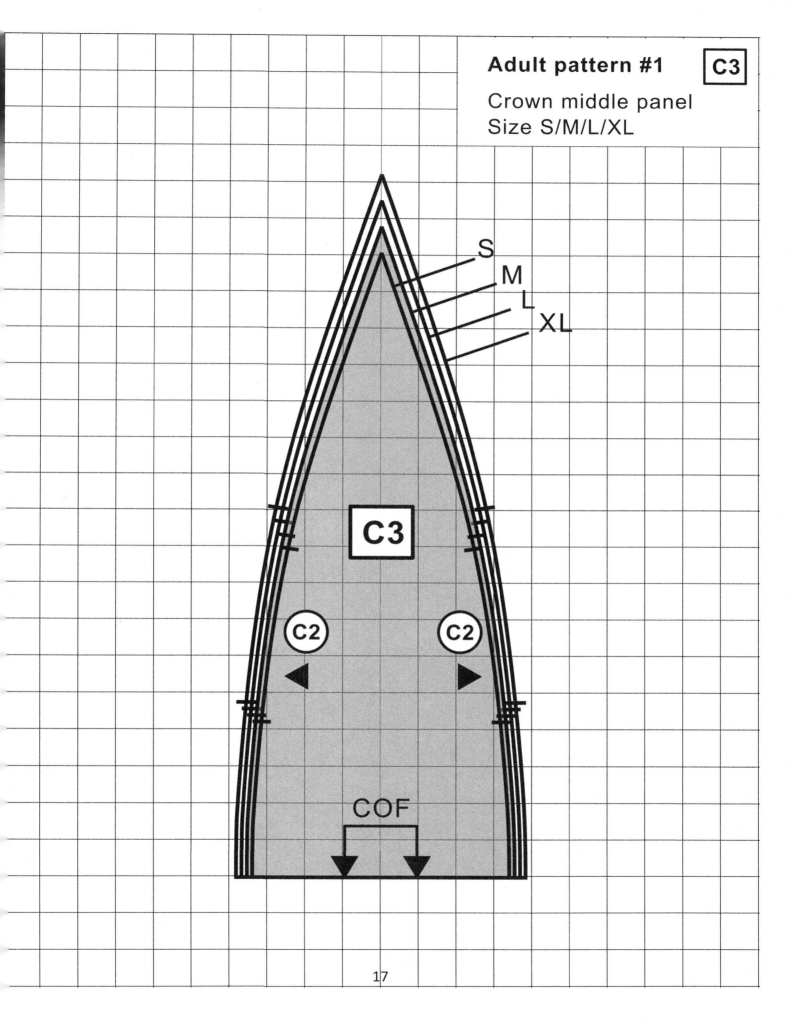

Adult pattern #1 C3

Crown middle panel
Size S/M/L/XL

S
M
L
XL

C3

C2   C2

COF

This page is intentionally blank

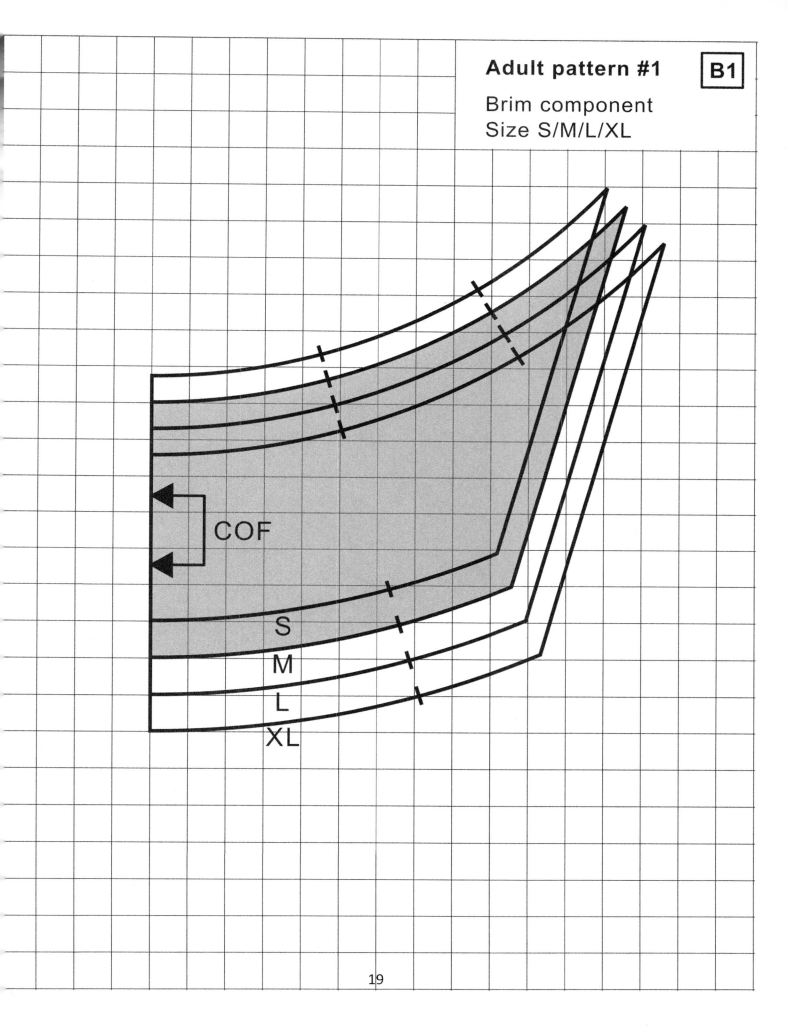

Adult pattern #1 B1

Brim component
Size S/M/L/XL

COF

S
M
L
XL

19

This page is intentionally blank

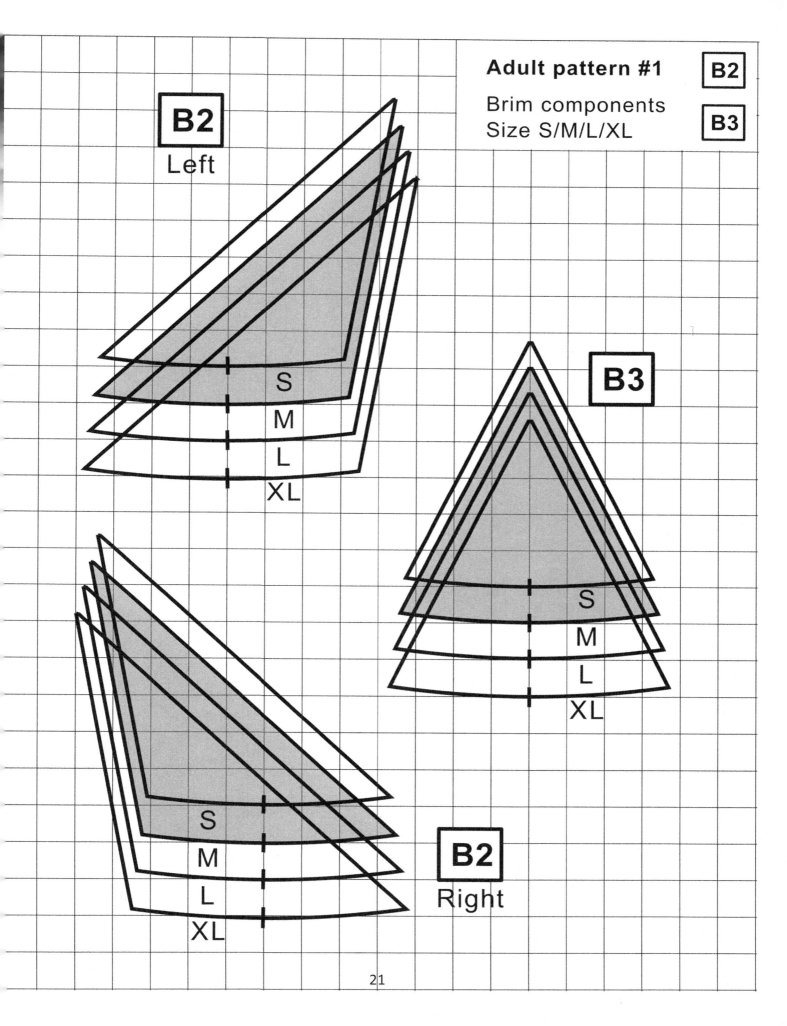

Adult pattern #1

Brim components
Size S/M/L/XL

B2

B3

B2 Left

S
M
L
XL

B3

S
M
L
XL

B2 Right

S
M
L
XL

This page is intentionally blank

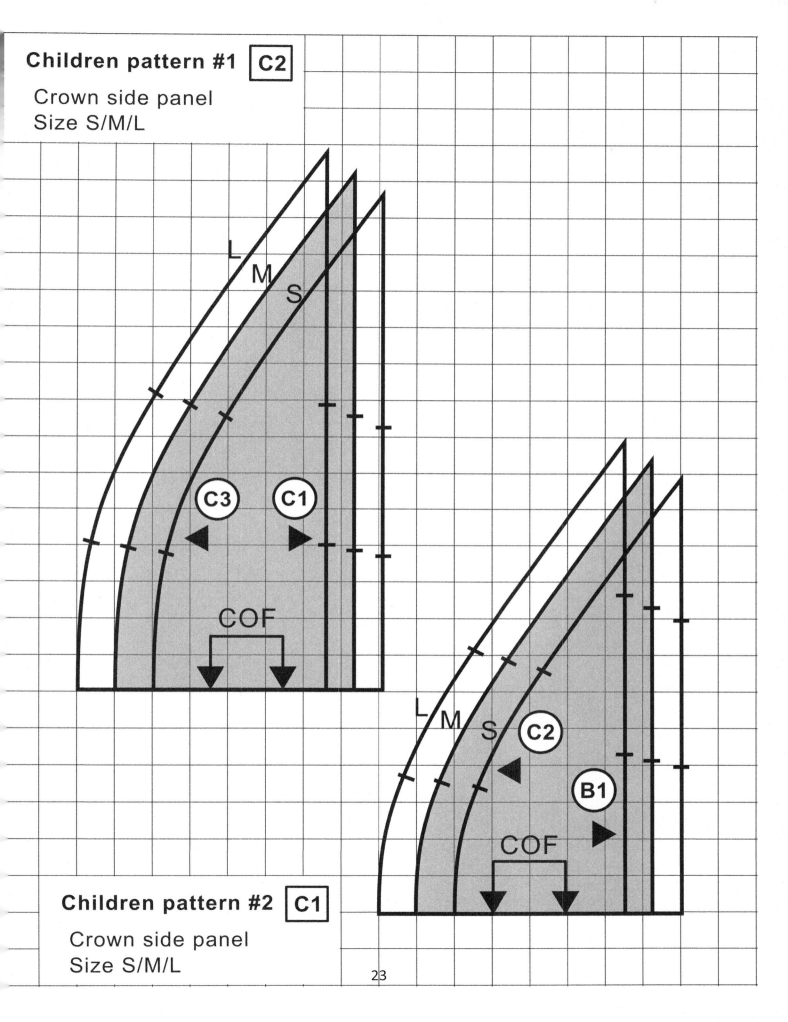

Children pattern #1 [C2]

Crown side panel
Size S/M/L

COF

Children pattern #2 [C1]

Crown side panel
Size S/M/L

23

This page is intentionally blank

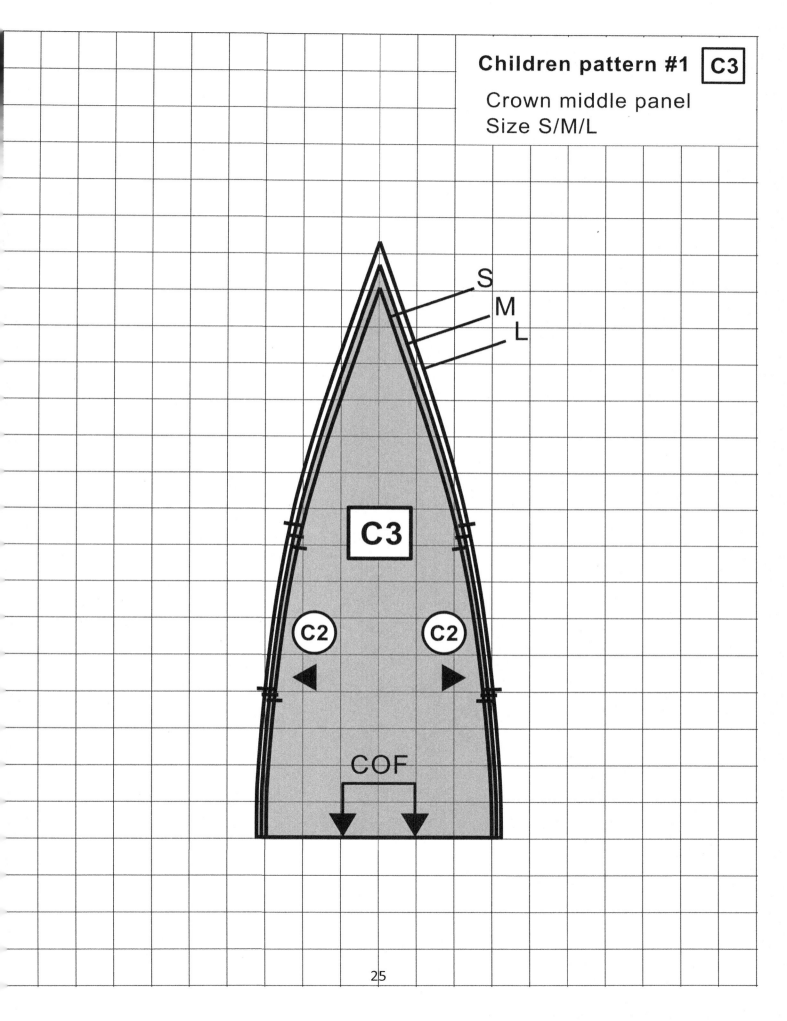

Children pattern #1 C3

Crown middle panel
Size S/M/L

S
M
L

C3

C2 C2

◄ ►

COF

25

This page is intentionally blank

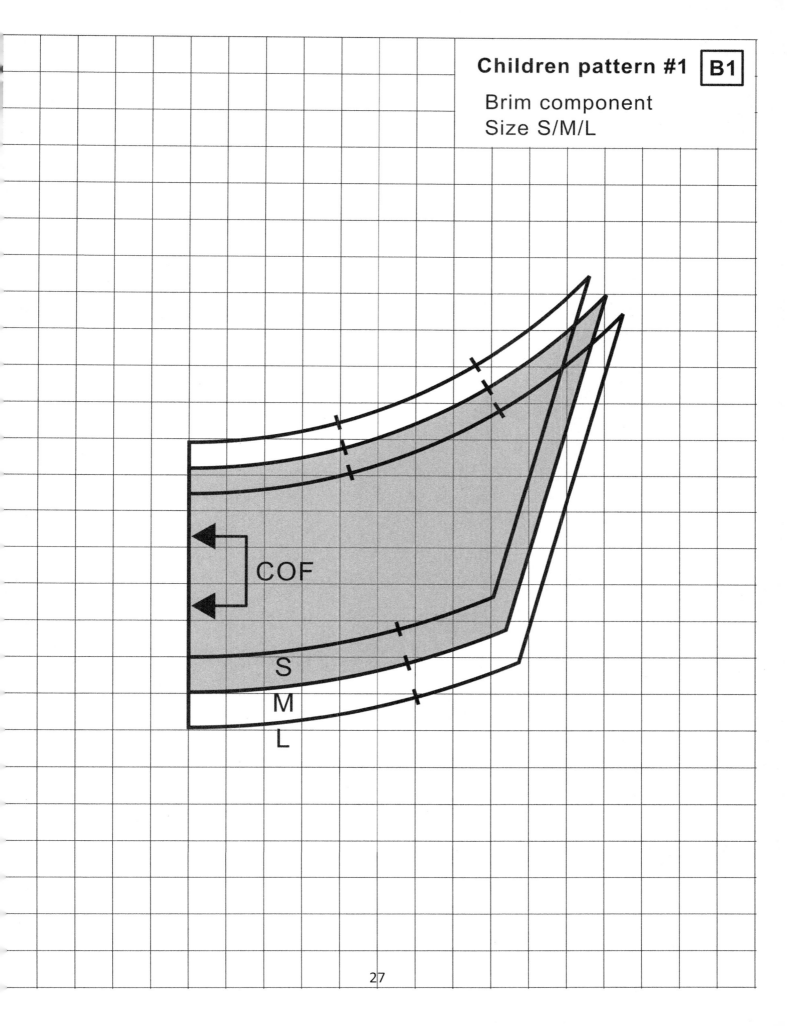

Children pattern #1 B1

Brim component
Size S/M/L

COF

S
M
L

27

This page is intentionally blank

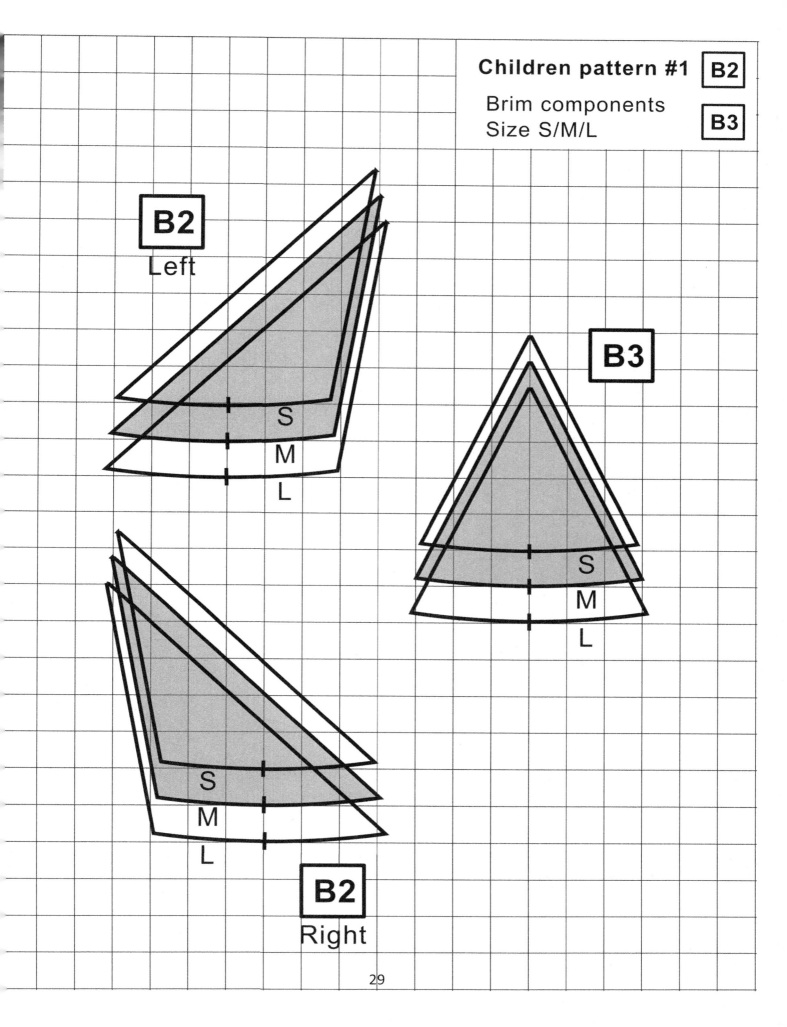

Children pattern #1   B2

Brim components   B3
Size S/M/L

B2
Left

S
M
L

B3

S
M
L

S
M
L

B2
Right

29

This page is intentionally blank

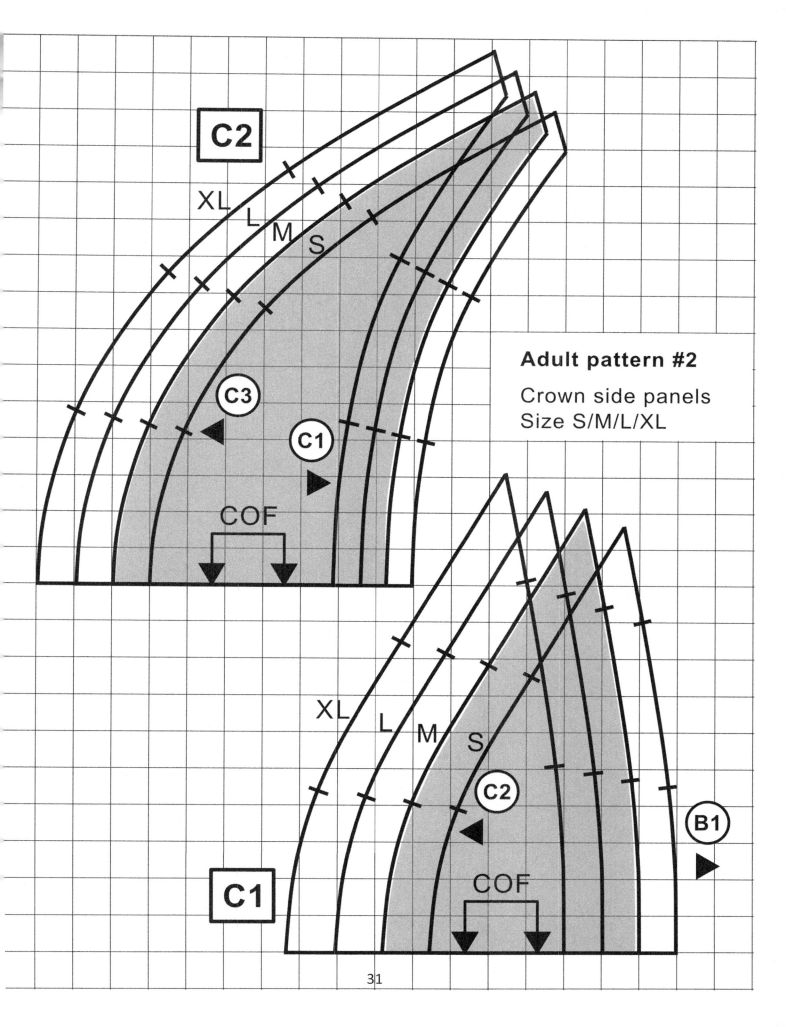

C2

XL
L
M
S

Adult pattern #2

Crown side panels
Size S/M/L/XL

C3

C1

COF

C1

XL
L
M
S

C2

B1

COF

31

This page is intentionally blank

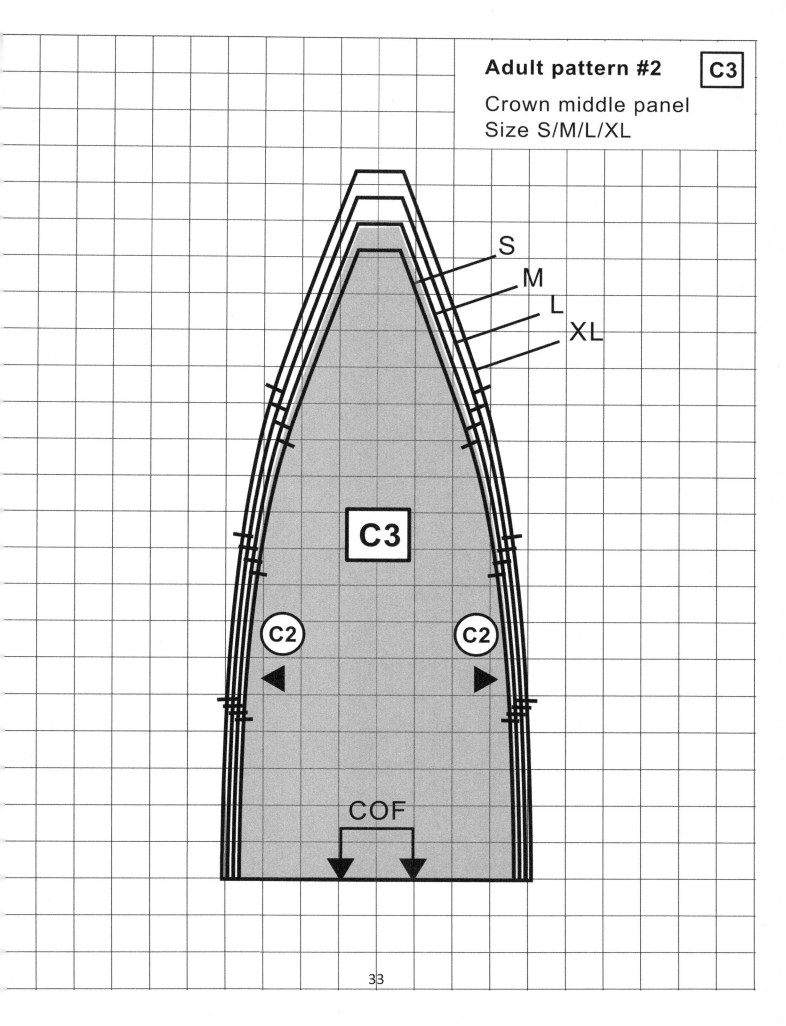

Adult pattern #2 C3

Crown middle panel
Size S/M/L/XL

S
M
L
XL

C3

C2 C2

◄ ►

COF

33

This page is intentionally blank

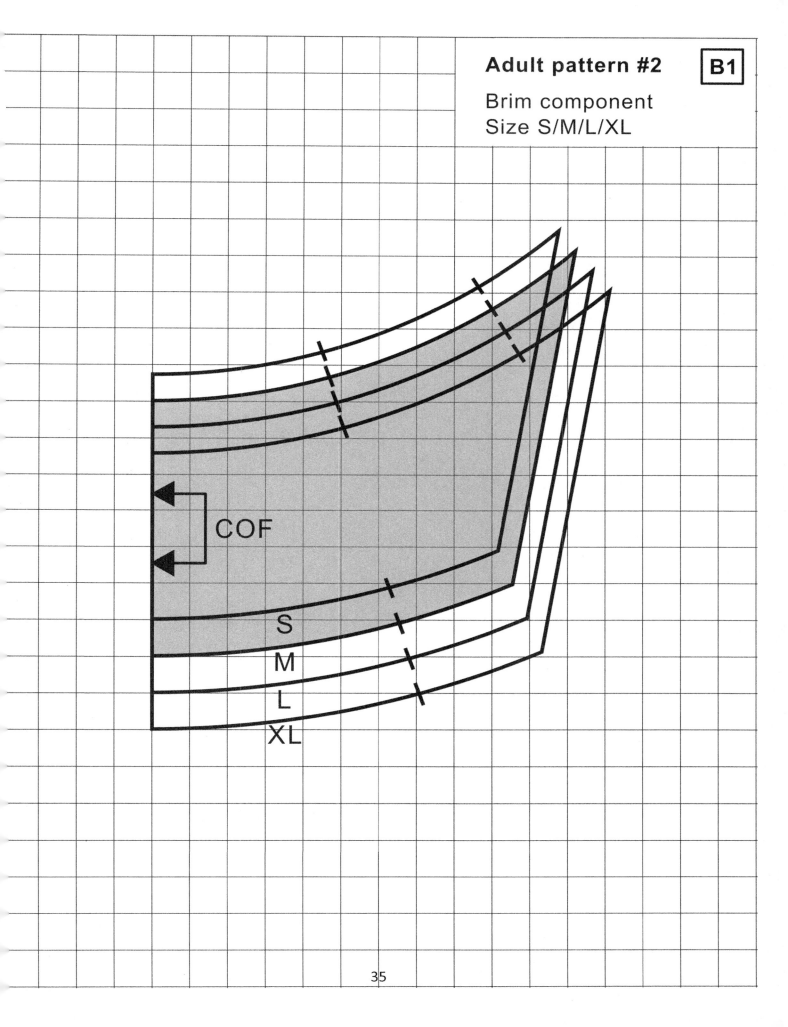

Adult pattern #2

B1

Brim component
Size S/M/L/XL

COF

S
M
L
XL

35

This page is intentionally blank

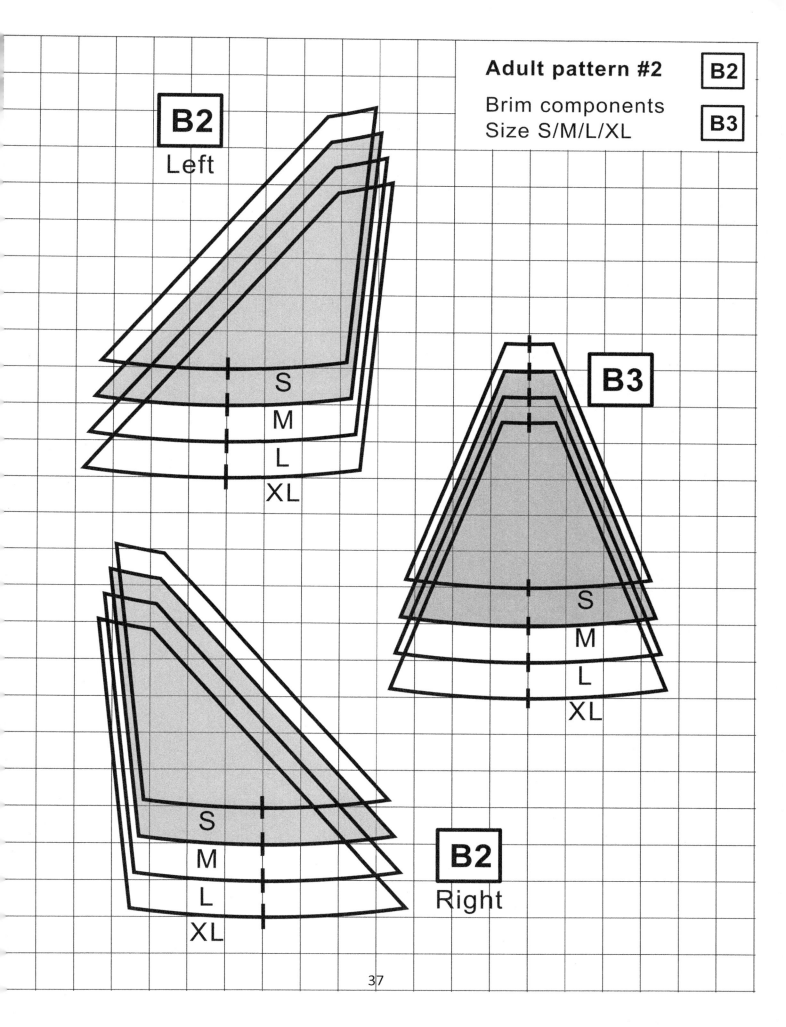

Adult pattern #2

Brim components
Size S/M/L/XL

B2
B3

B2
Left

S
M
L
XL

B3

S
M
L
XL

B2
Right

S
M
L
XL

This page is intentionally blank

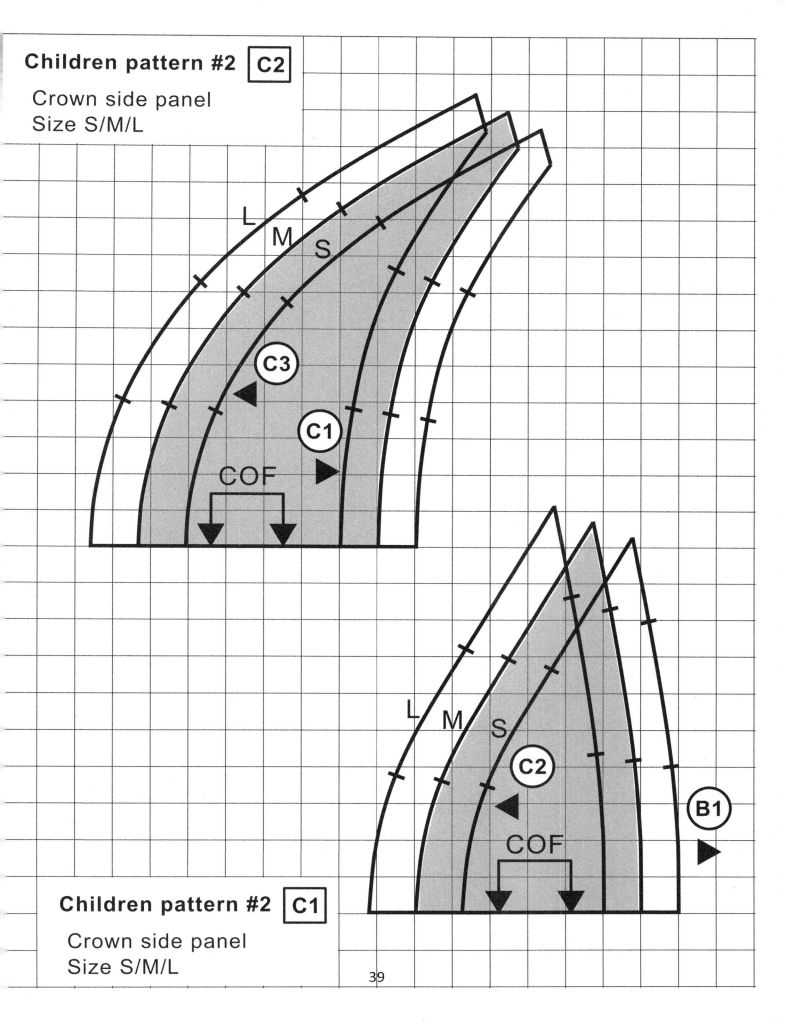

Children pattern #2 [C2]

Crown side panel
Size S/M/L

L M S

C3

C1

COF

Children pattern #2 [C1]

Crown side panel
Size S/M/L

L M S

C2

B1

COF

This page is intentionally blank

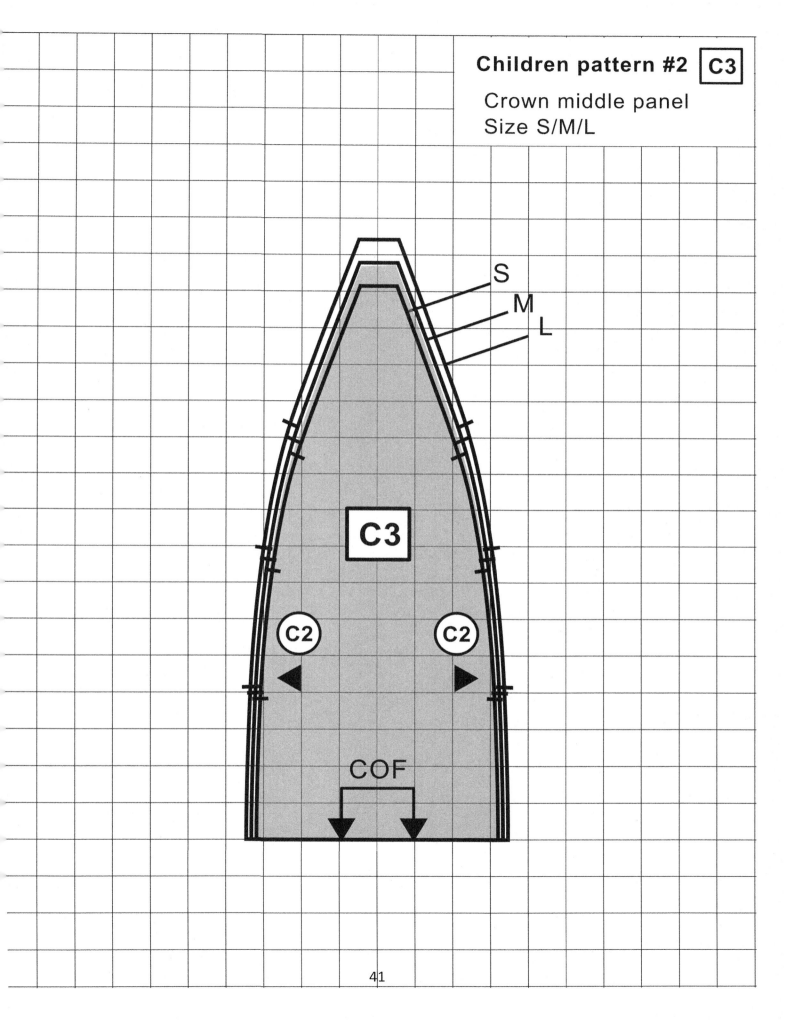

Children pattern #2 C3

Crown middle panel
Size S/M/L

S
M
L

C3

C2   C2

COF

This page is intentionally blank

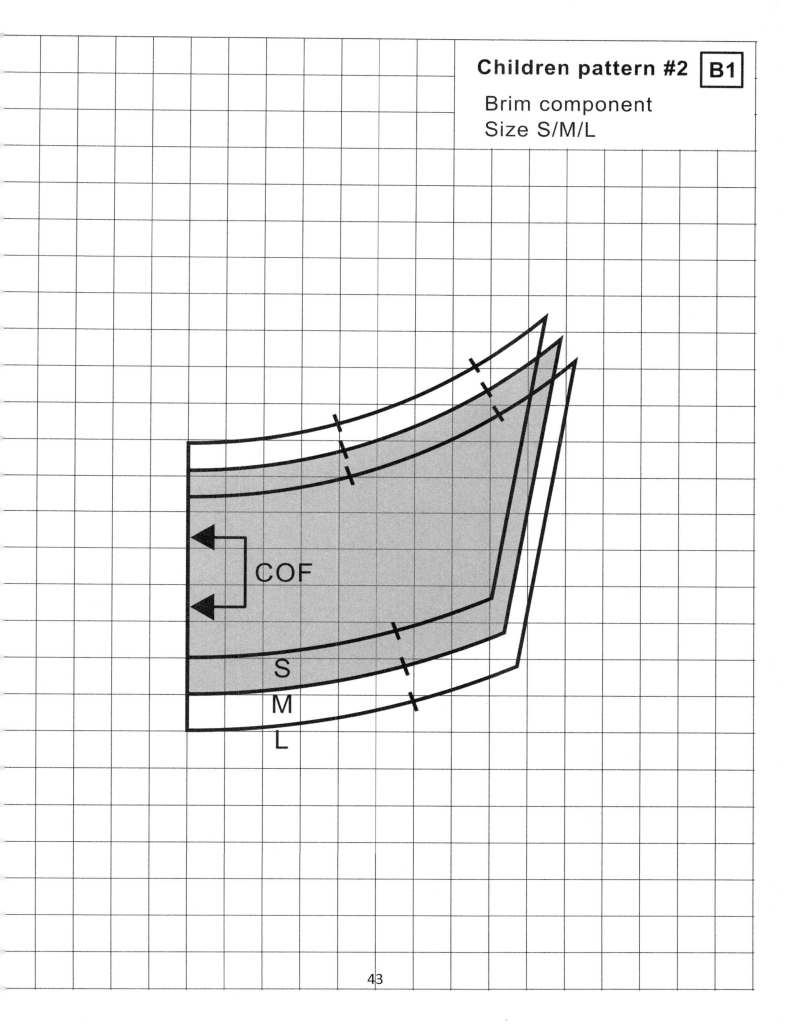

Children pattern #2 **B1**

Brim component
Size S/M/L

COF

S
M
L

This page is intentionally blank

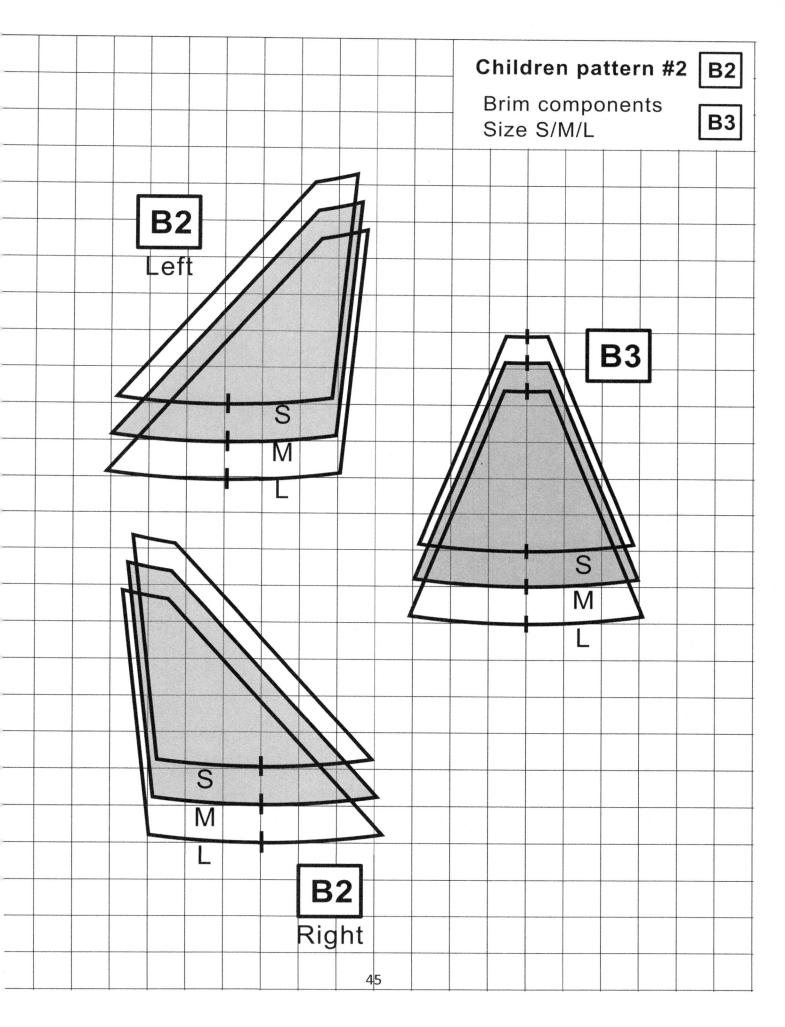

Children pattern #2   B2

Brim components   B3
Size S/M/L

B2
Left

B3

S
M
L

S
M
L

B2
Right

S
M
L

45

This page is intentionally blank

Creative circuit hat patterns #3

- Provided are patterns size S/M/L/XL for adults, and S/M/L for children.

- As multiple sizes are displayed on the same pages, only size M is gray shaded, in order to ease the reading.

- **T0, S1** and **S2** shall be used, for the top and side panels of the crown, respectively. For each layer of the two side-panel circuits, 3 pieces from 3 different fabrics in a certain cyclic order will be needed.

- For lining, either flipped **S1** and **S2**, or symmetrical **L1** and **L2**, shall be used. In case of the latter, depending on your preference, you may choose to make 3 separated pieces to join together later (perhaps, from your left-overs), or just one full panel (from a bigger piece of fabric).

- For the brim and underbrim, there are two options to choose from; **B1** or **B2**. In either option, 3 pieces will be needed to make one. For **B2**, a flipped template is required to make the underbrim.

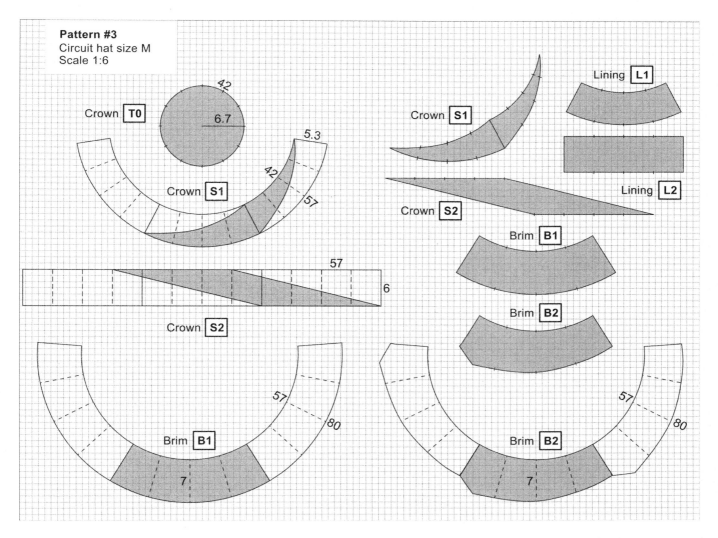

Materials

- Fabrics #1, #2, and #3 for each set of the crown side (**S1**, **S2**), and under brim (**B1**, or **flipped B2**)

- Fabric #4 for the crown top (**T0**), and brim (**B1** or **B2**)

- Fabric #5 for lining (**T0, flipped S1, flipped S2**) or (**T0, L1, L2**)

- Depending on the fabrics used, making one hat will generally require less than a yard of fabric.

- A sweatband with length equal to your head circumference, plus seam allowance (SA), that circles completely inside the crown at its base will be also needed. You may choose from some leftovers to create one on your own (i.e., a non-bias strip for 2-3 cm wide binding).

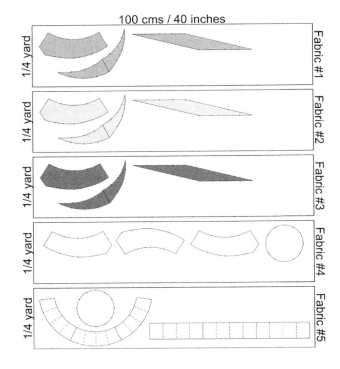

100 cms / 40 inches

1/4 yard — Fabric #1
1/4 yard — Fabric #2
1/4 yard — Fabric #3
1/4 yard — Fabric #4
1/4 yard — Fabric #5

- Interface (i.e., iron-on stabilizer), to insert inside the brim, is optional. You don't need any if the fabrics are thick and stiff enough. To prepare the interface, use the same brim template <u>with</u> SA.

- Also, if desired, wadding can be added, to create another soft fluffy layer to be sandwiched between the outer fabrics, and probably with extra texture by stitching multiple rows around. To prepare wadding, use the same brim template <u>with</u> SA.

- Please note some comments about grain line in the introduction section.

Construction

- **The crown** – Match the seams to sew 3 panels of **S1** to form a loop. You shall clip along SA to relax tension and ease the alignment of the curved seams. Do similarly for **S2**. Then, put the right sides of the circuit **S1** and **S2** layers together, and match the seam to sew and form a wider loop. (You may try rotating one layer around another, and let your eyes decide the aesthetic spot to pause.) Trim off and/or clip along SA as appropriate (beware not to snip the thread). After that, join **T0** at the top, to finish out the crown. Do the same for lining. Then put their wrong sides together, match the bottom seams and stitch on the right side below the intended circumference line to lock them together.

- **The brim** – Stick the interface to each brim panel. Sew 3 panels together to form a loop. Do the same for the underbrim. For the seams not to be too thick, do seam grading by trimming off a portion of SA on the interface, and/or the underbrim. Then put their right sides together, and match the outer seams to sew. Trim off and/or clip along the SA, turn the right sides out, and make single or double edge stitching.

- **Assembly** – Put the right sides of the crown and brim components together and match the crown-brim seams. Additional clipping along SA would be needed to relax tension and ease the alignment (especially on the concave seam of the brim), before sewing them together. Then you may (or may not) do overlock stitching for tidiness reason. Finally, align the sweatband to the combined seam and stitch over to complete your circuit hat.

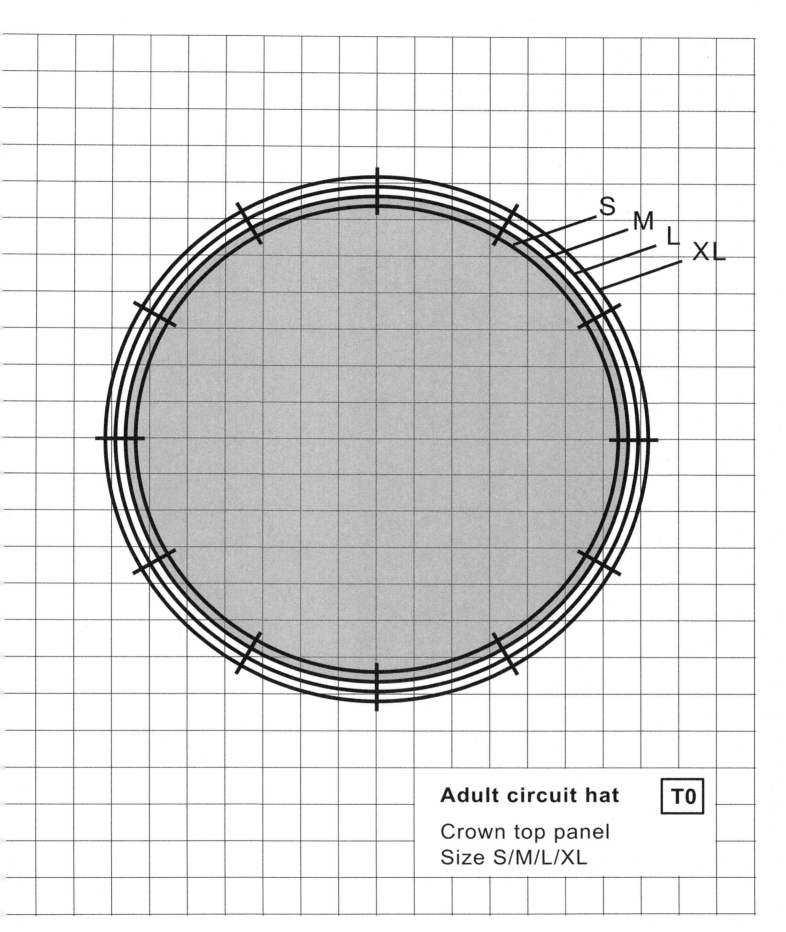

Adult circuit hat `T0`

Crown top panel
Size S/M/L/XL

This page is intentionally blank

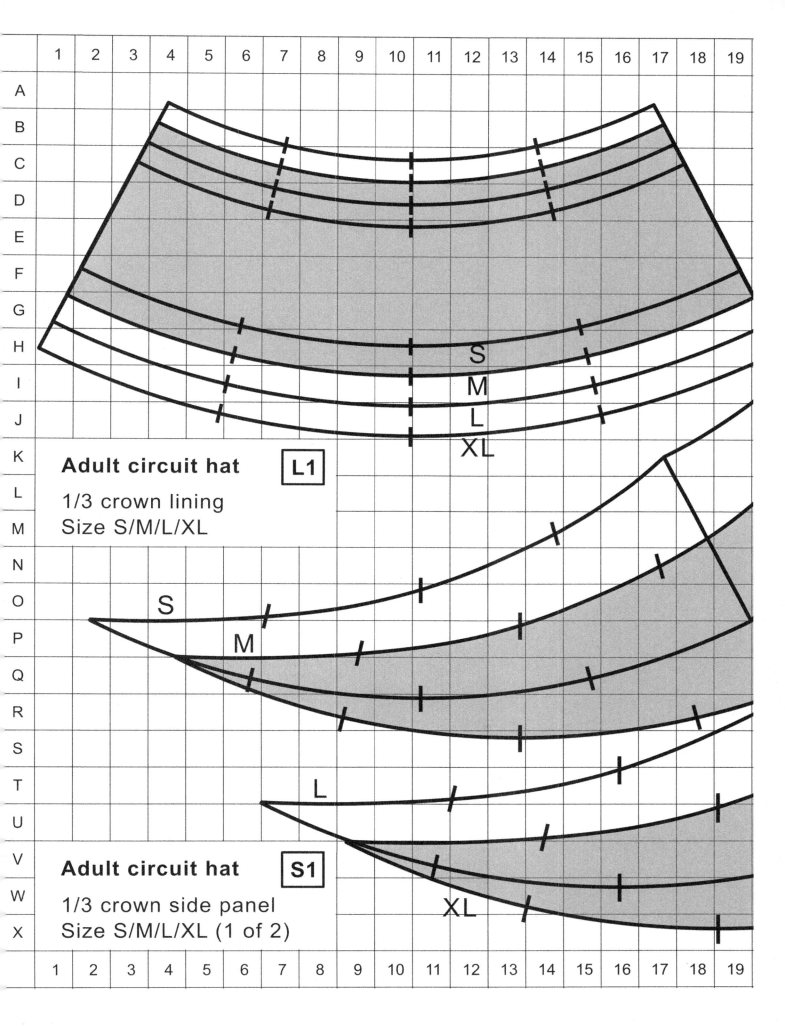

Adult circuit hat L1

1/3 crown lining
Size S/M/L/XL

S
M
L
XL

Adult circuit hat S1

1/3 crown side panel
Size S/M/L/XL (1 of 2)

S
M
L
XL

This page is intentionally blank

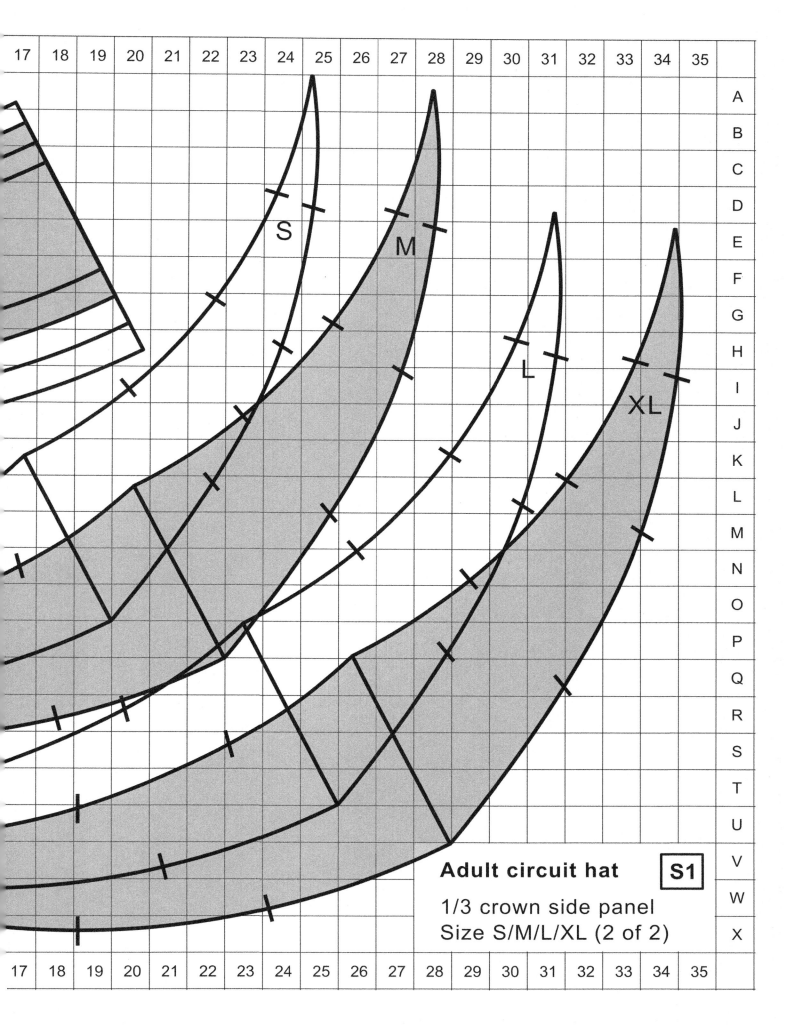

Adult circuit hat S1

1/3 crown side panel
Size S/M/L/XL (2 of 2)

This page is intentionally blank

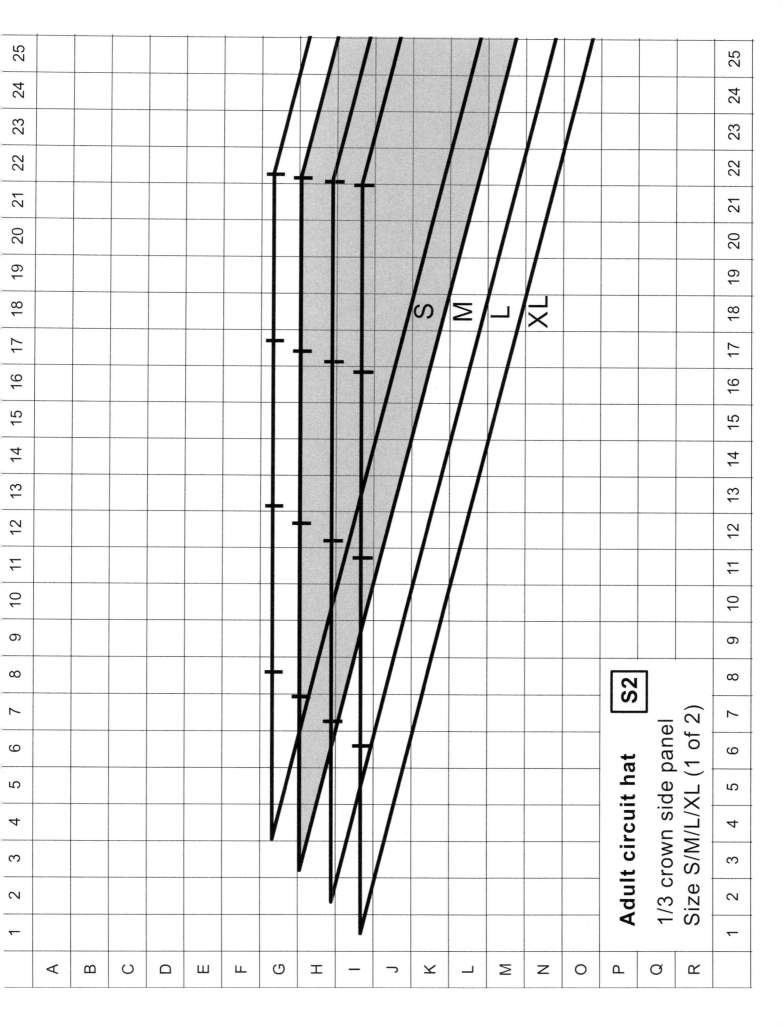

Adult circuit hat

1/3 crown side panel
Size S/M/L/XL (1 of 2)

S2

This page is intentionally blank

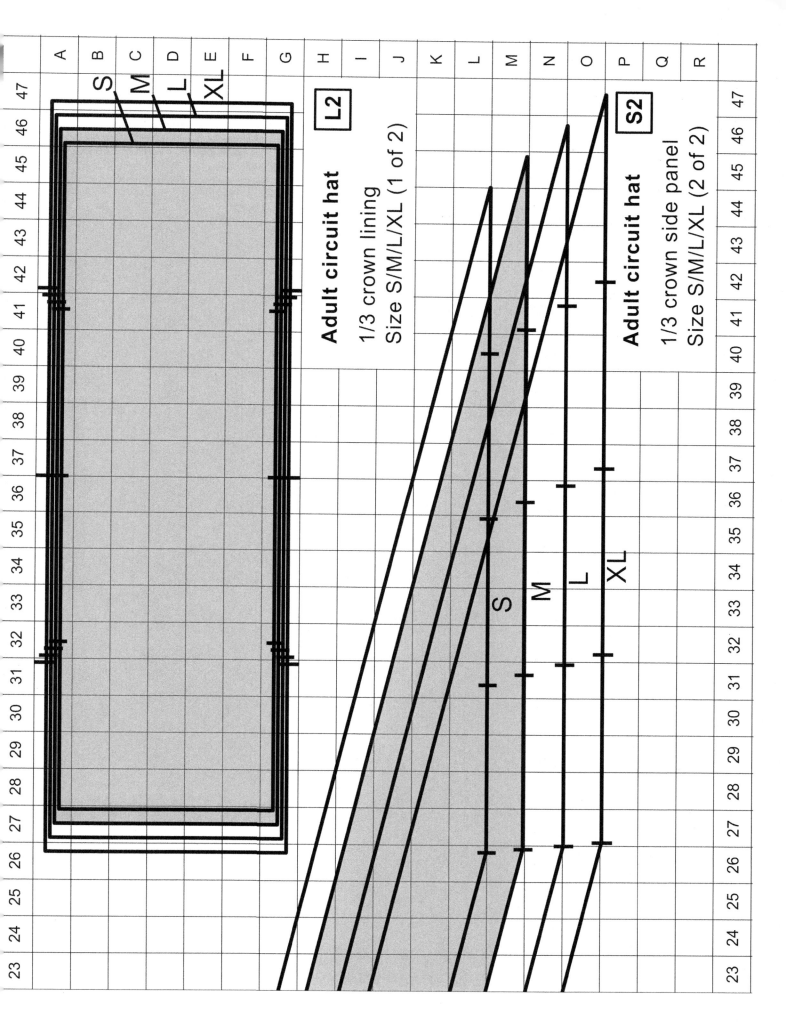

Adult circuit hat

1/3 crown lining
Size S/M/L/XL (1 of 2)

L2

Adult circuit hat

1/3 crown side panel
Size S/M/L/XL (2 of 2)

S2

This page is intentionally blank

	1	2	3	4	5	6	7	8	9	10	11	12	13	14	15	16	17	18	19
A																			
B																			
C																			
D																			
E																			
F																			
G																			
H																			
I																			
J																			
K																			
L																			
M																			
N																			
O																			
P																			
Q																			
R																			
S																			
T																			
U																			
V																			
W																			
X																			

Adult circuit hat B1

1/3 brim option 1
Size S/M/L/XL (1 of 2)

S
M
L
XL

This page is intentionally blank

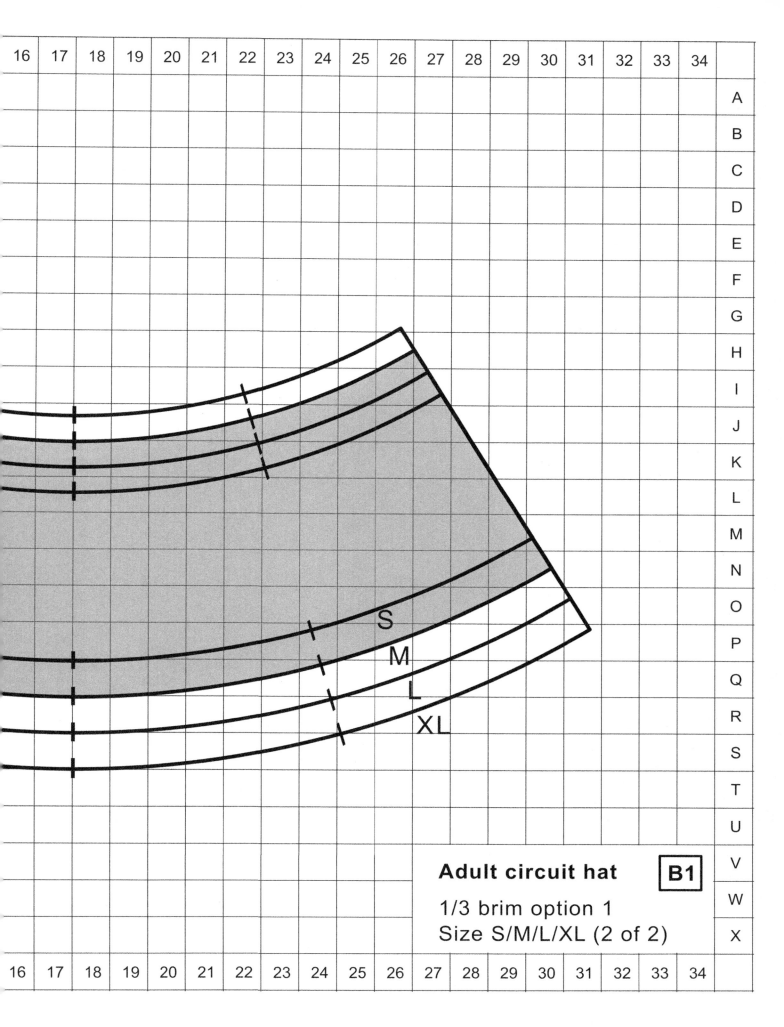

Adult circuit hat B1

1/3 brim option 1
Size S/M/L/XL (2 of 2)

This page is intentionally blank

Adult circuit hat B2

1/3 brim option 2
Size S/M/L/XL (1 of 2)

S

M

L

XL

This page is intentionally blank

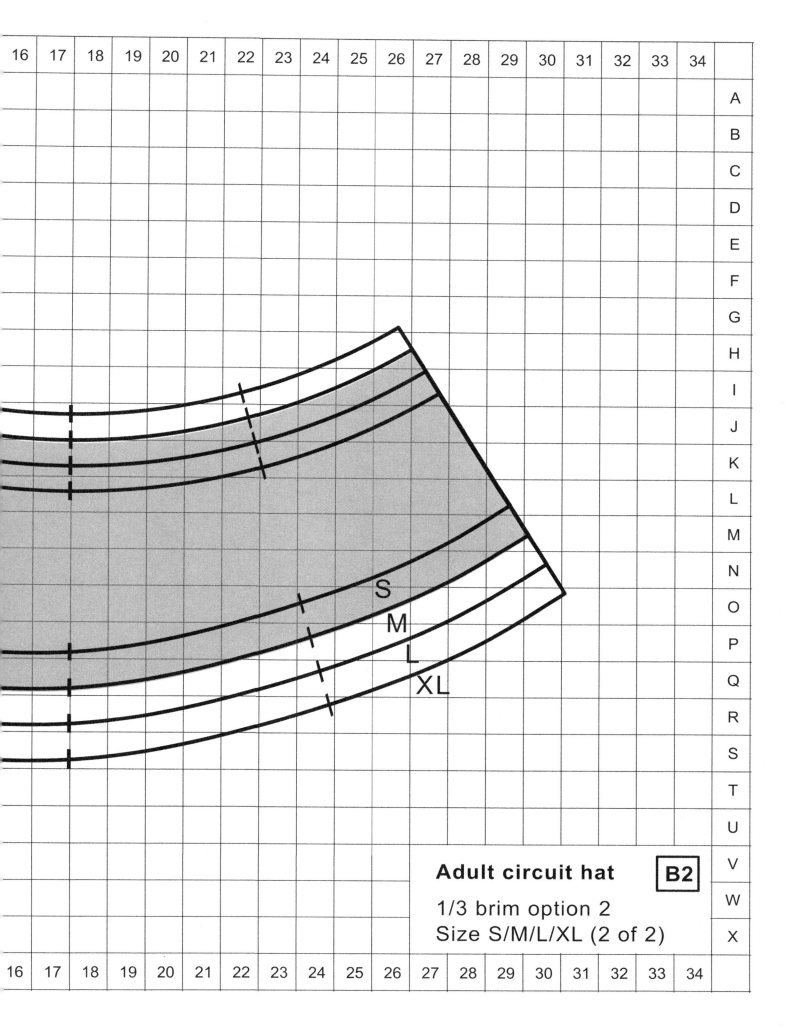

Adult circuit hat **B2**

1/3 brim option 2
Size S/M/L/XL (2 of 2)

This page is intentionally blank

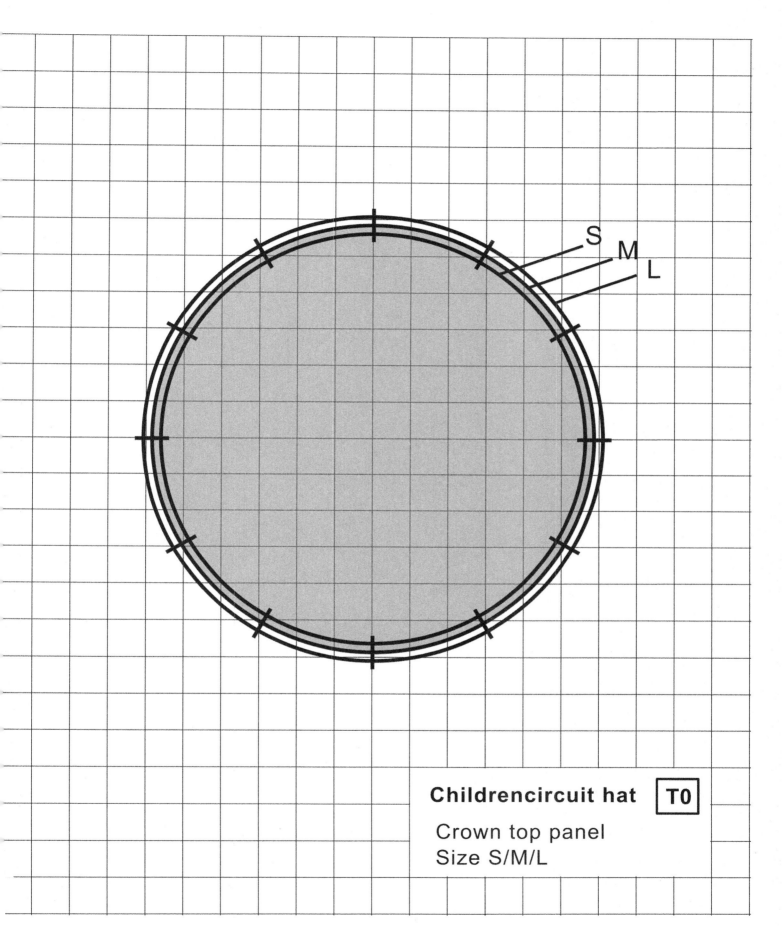

Childrencircuit hat T0

Crown top panel
Size S/M/L

This page is intentionally blank

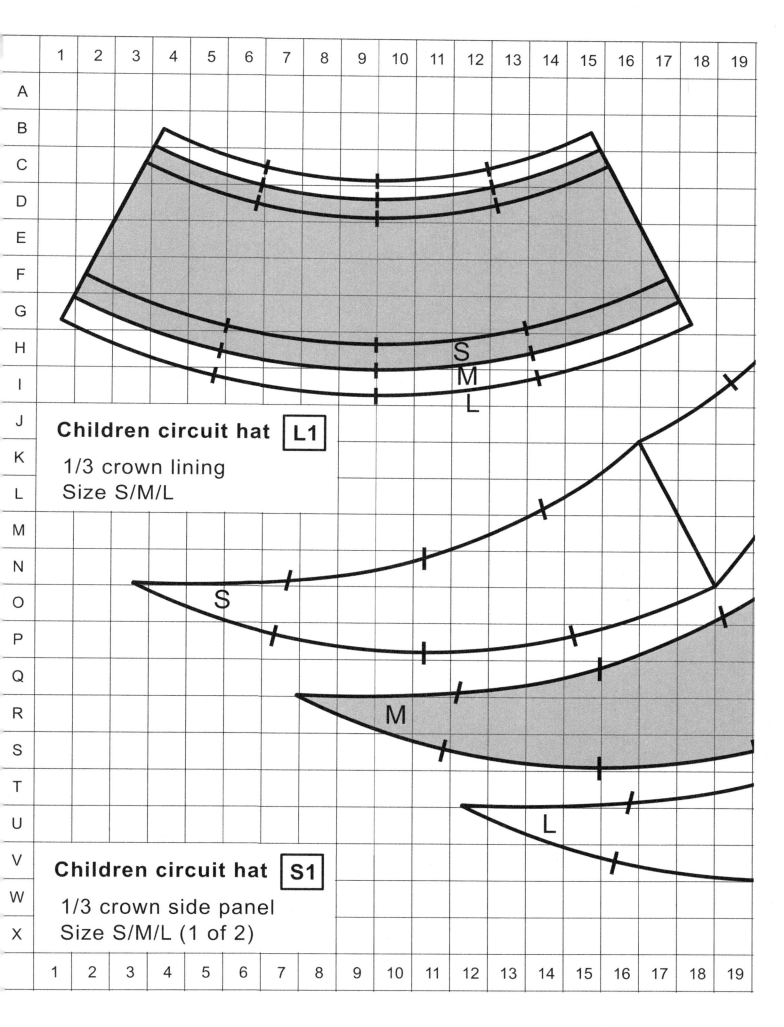

Children circuit hat L1

1/3 crown lining
Size S/M/L

Children circuit hat S1

1/3 crown side panel
Size S/M/L (1 of 2)

This page is intentionally blank

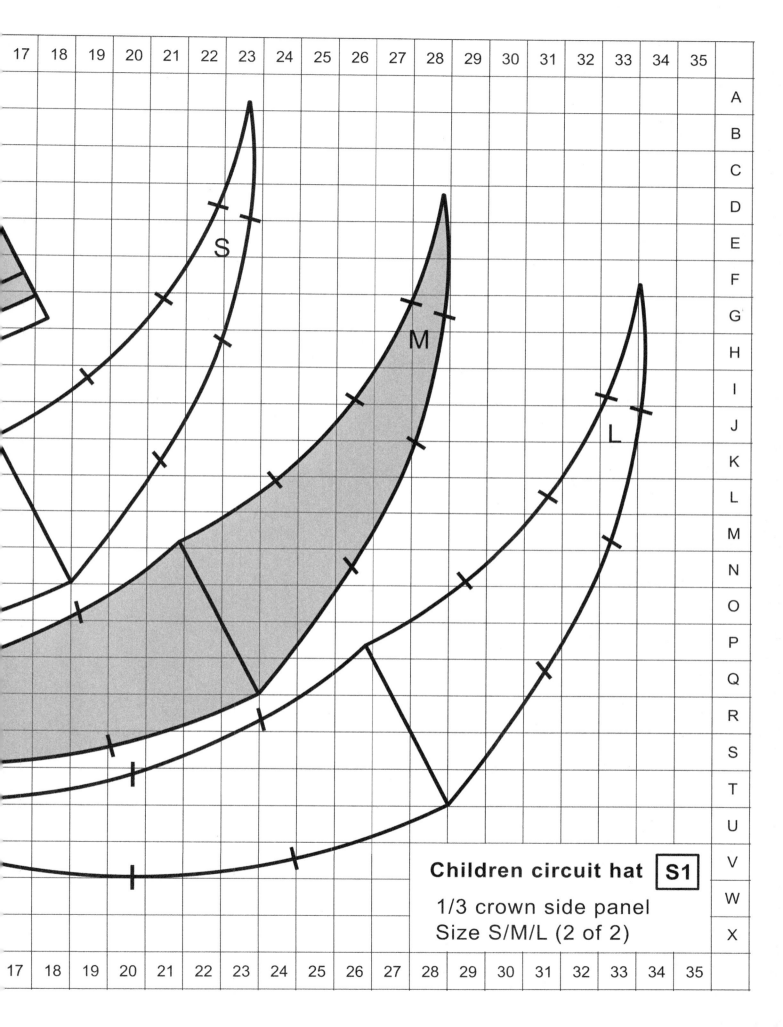

Children circuit hat S1

1/3 crown side panel
Size S/M/L (2 of 2)

This page is intentionally blank

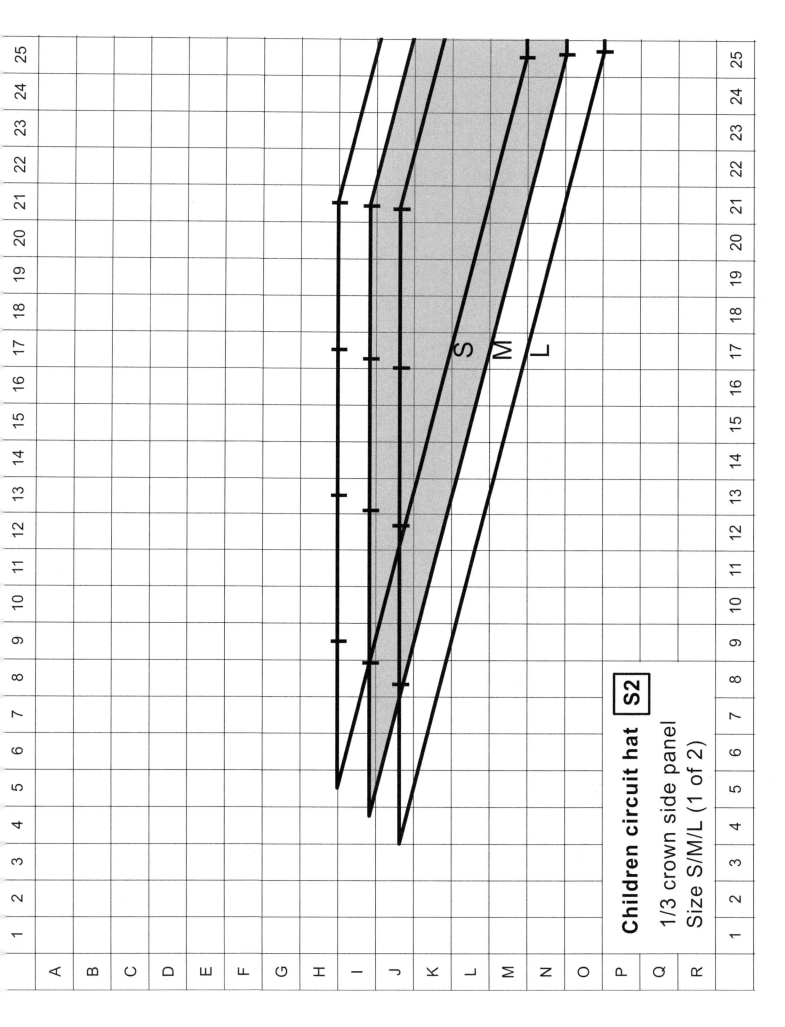

Children circuit hat S2

1/3 crown side panel
Size S/M/L (1 of 2)

This page is intentionally blank

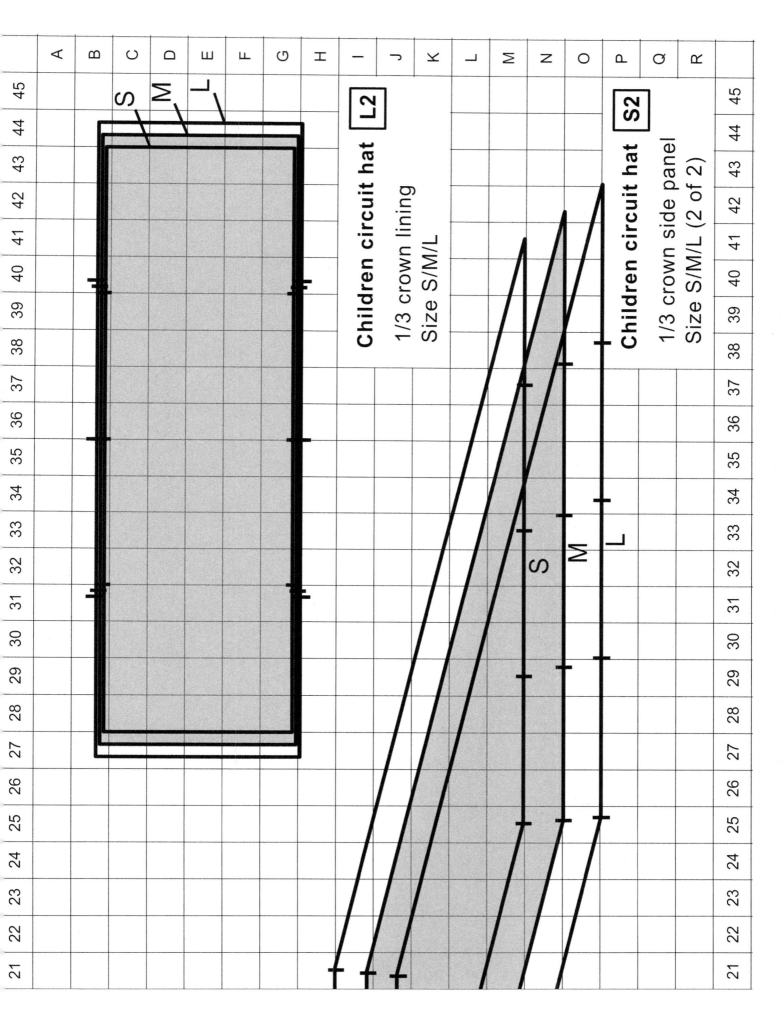

Children circuit hat L2

1/3 crown lining
Size S/M/L

Children circuit hat S2

1/3 crown side panel
Size S/M/L (2 of 2)

This page is intentionally blank

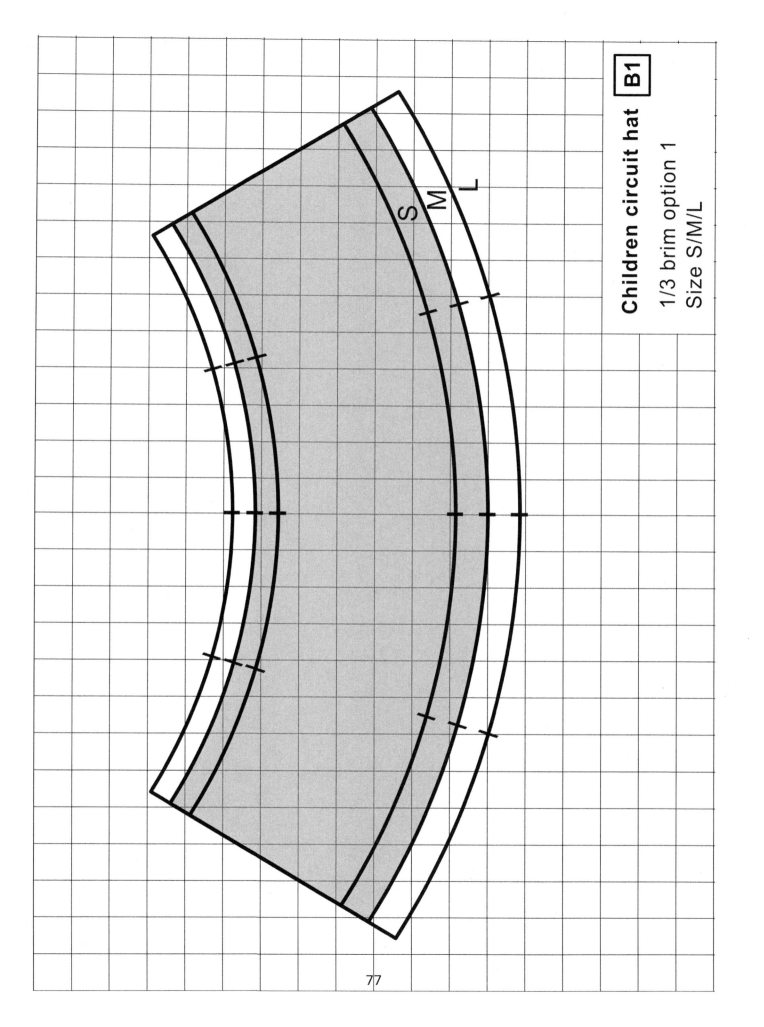

Children circuit hat B1

1/3 brim option 1

Size S/M/L

S

M

L

77

This page is intentionally blank

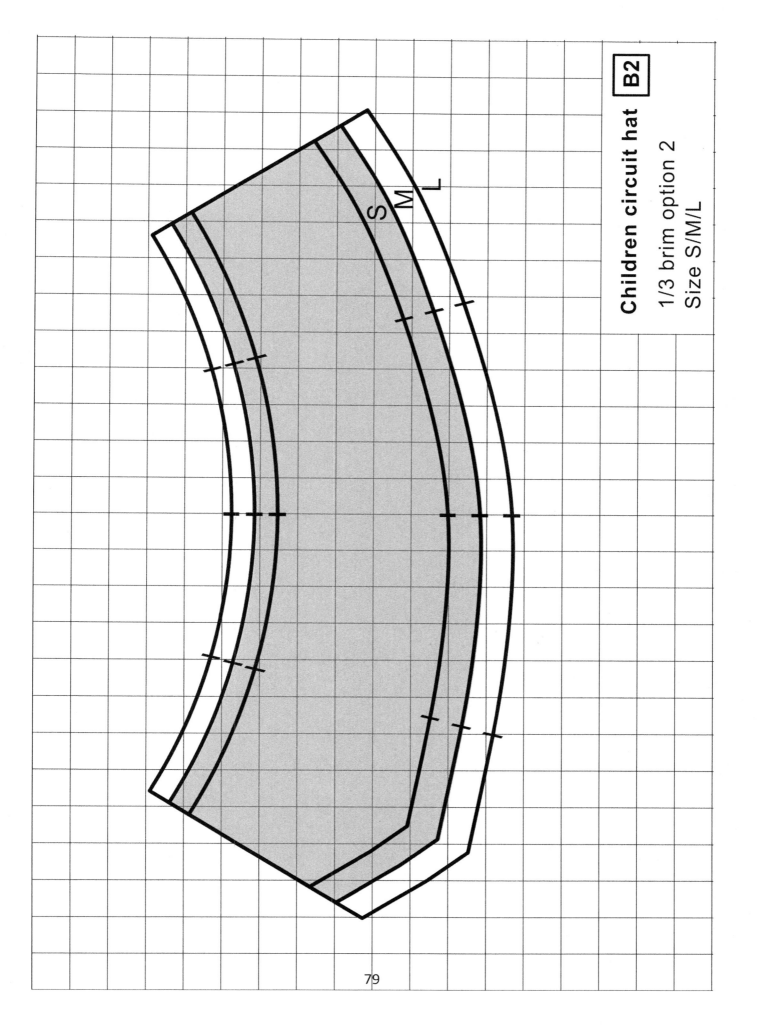

Children circuit hat B2
1/3 brim option 2
Size S/M/L

S
M
L

This page is intentionally blank

Creative spiral hat patterns #4

- Provided are patterns size S/M/L/XL for adults, and S/M/L for children.

- Only size M is gray shaded, in order to ease the reading.

- For the actual size template are made separately the crown and brim. Six pieces for each template will be needed to make one.

- However, you may also choose to join them together (before adding SA), and have another option (called **Option #2**, as below) with the combined crown-brim for each single panel. This option is easier, and give a quick way to make a reversible hat.

- It is recommended to use the same option for both the outer and inner components. Although, mixing the two options is possible and interesting (for example, **Option #1** for outer, and **Option #2** for inner), extra wrinkles caused by small volume mismatch around the crown base can be seen on the side with **Option #2**.

- A flipped template is required to make the underbrim, lining, or the inner component in case of a reversible hat.

- For **Option #2**, hem binding with bias strip can be used for finishing. In this case, it's possible not to spare SA on the bottom edge.

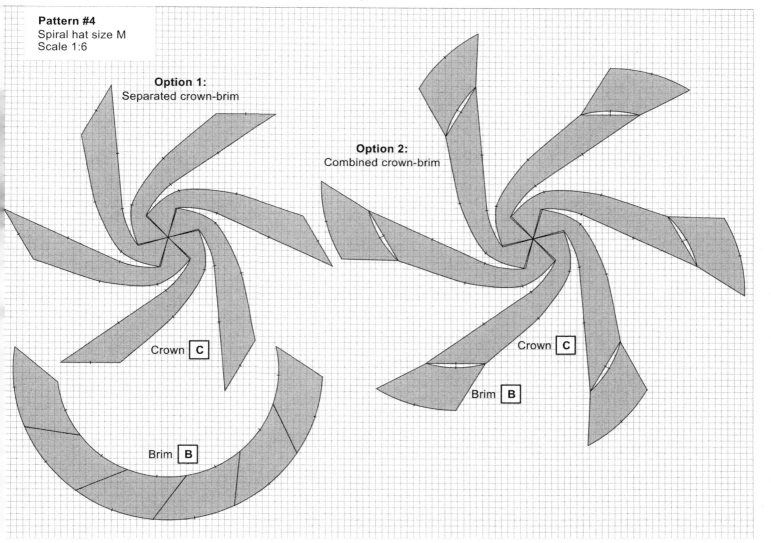

Pattern #4
Spiral hat size M
Scale 1:6

Option 1:
Separated crown-brim

Option 2:
Combined crown-brim

Crown C

Brim B

Crown C

Brim B

Materials

- You are free to plan for the mix-and-match of fabrics and/or left-overs. All six panels can be made from 2, 3, or 6 different fabric mix.

- A sweatband with length equal to your head circumference, plus seam allowance (SA) is only needed in case of a single-sided hat in **Option #1**.

- Interface (i.e., iron-on stabilizer) is optional for the brim portion. You don't need any if the fabrics are thick and stiff enough. A brim template with SA are used to prepare the interface. In case of a reversible hat, the interface is to be sticked to the brim part of either the outer or inner component.

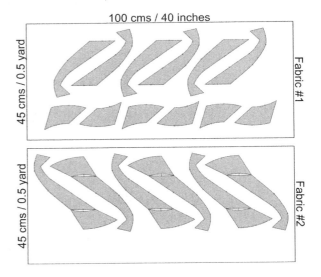

- Also, if desired, wadding can be added. To prepare, use the same brim template <u>with</u> SA.

- A bias strip (which can be made from the same fabric of about 90-cm length for adult size M, plus/minus 4-cm for every sizing step up/down) is required for hem finishing in **Option #2**.

- Please note some comments about grain line and corner sewing in the introduction section.

Construction

- Stick the interface and/or wadding to the brim. If the brim is separated (as in **Option #1**), join all panels into a loop, following the desired sequence of fabric mix. And do the same for underbrim. In case of a reversible hat in **Option #2**, top-edge stitching is required to lock the interface to the brim, before trimming off excess SA of the interface (beware not to snip the thread and crown-brim fabrics).

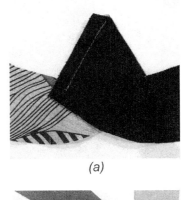

(a)

- For the crown, sew a small portion from the top down to the first corner point to join any two pieces together (a). Do the same to join the third piece, and keep them as the first set. Repeat the same for another 3-panel set. Then, align well (especially at the top tip) and sew these two sets together. All 6 panels are joined now (b). Do the same for lining, or the inner component.

- Match rest of the seam for each pair, follow corner sewing instructions provided earlier, and sew from the first corner down to the crown base for **Option #1**, or to the brim edge for **Option #2**.

(b)

- **Assembly** – For **Option #1**, you can do the same as in other designs; combine the crown and lining, combine the brim and underbrim (plus multiple row stitching, if desired), and join the two components together before finishing with a sweatband.

- **Hem finishing** – For **Option #2**, align the hem, do loose stitching to lock the inner and outer components together, before making bias strip binding to finish out the hem. To stitch multiple rows around, make sure that the brim and underbrim's fabrics are kept as smooth as possible to each other.

Adult spiral hat C

1/6 crown template
Size S/M/L/XL (1 of 2)

This page is intentionally blank

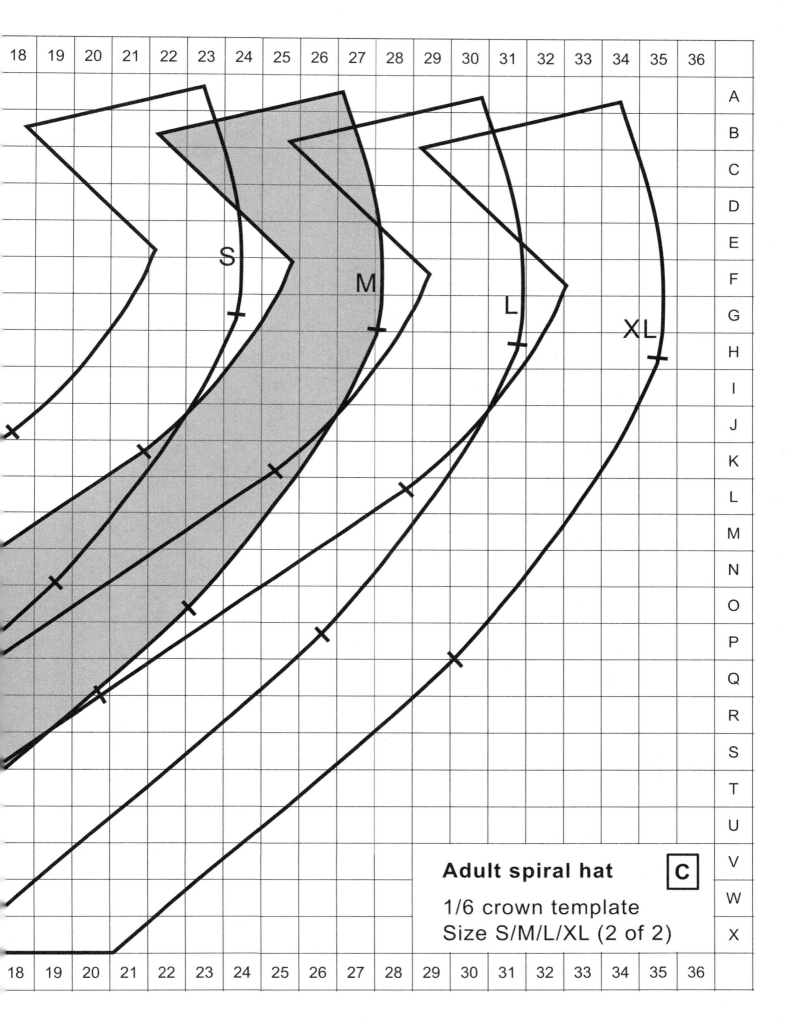

Adult spiral hat C

1/6 crown template
Size S/M/L/XL (2 of 2)

This page is intentionally blank

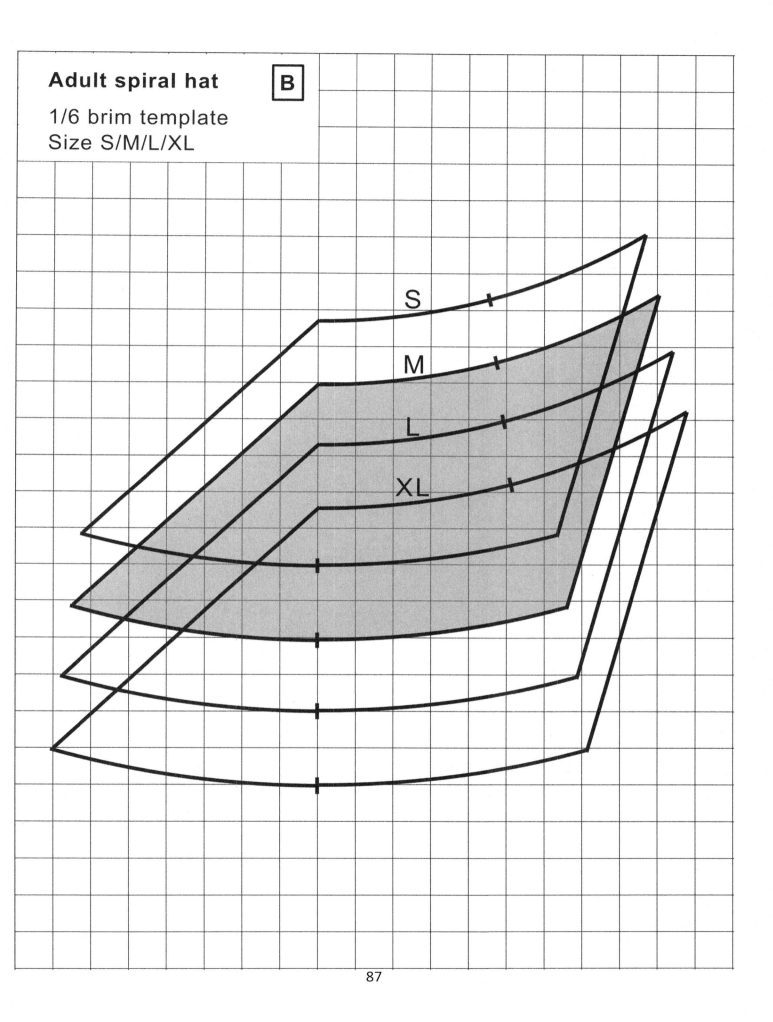

Adult spiral hat B

1/6 brim template
Size S/M/L/XL

S

M

L

XL

This page is intentionally blank

Children spiral hat C

1/6 crown template
Size S/M/L (1 of 2)

S

M

L

This page is intentionally blank

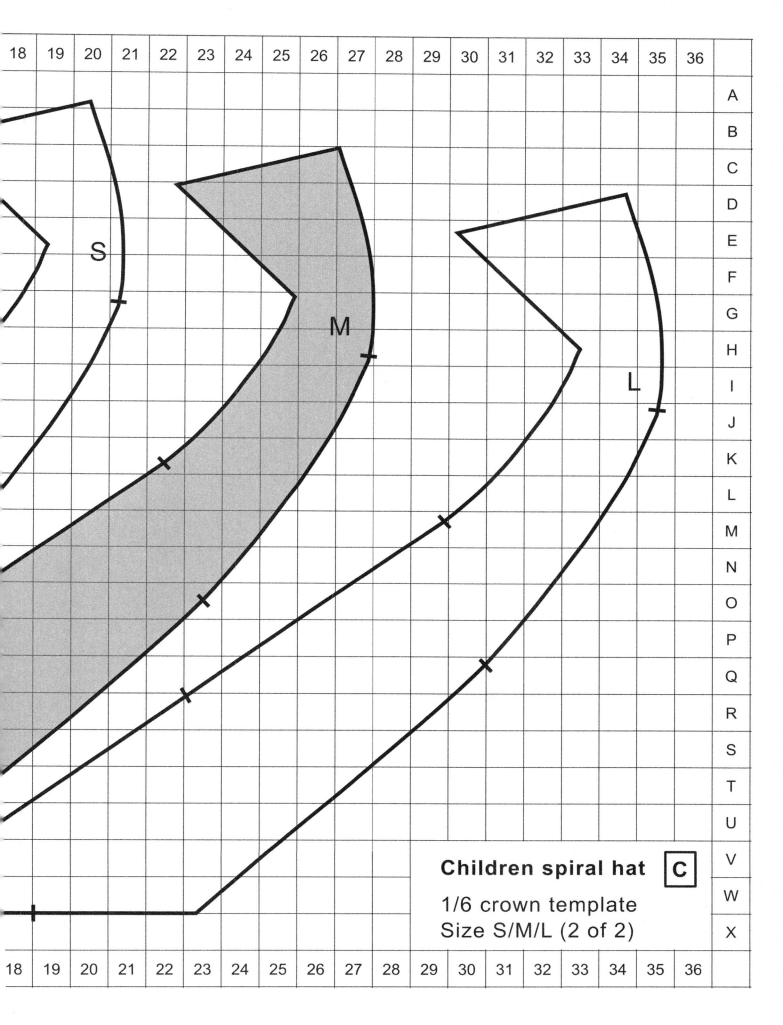

Children spiral hat [C]

1/6 crown template
Size S/M/L (2 of 2)

This page is intentionally blank

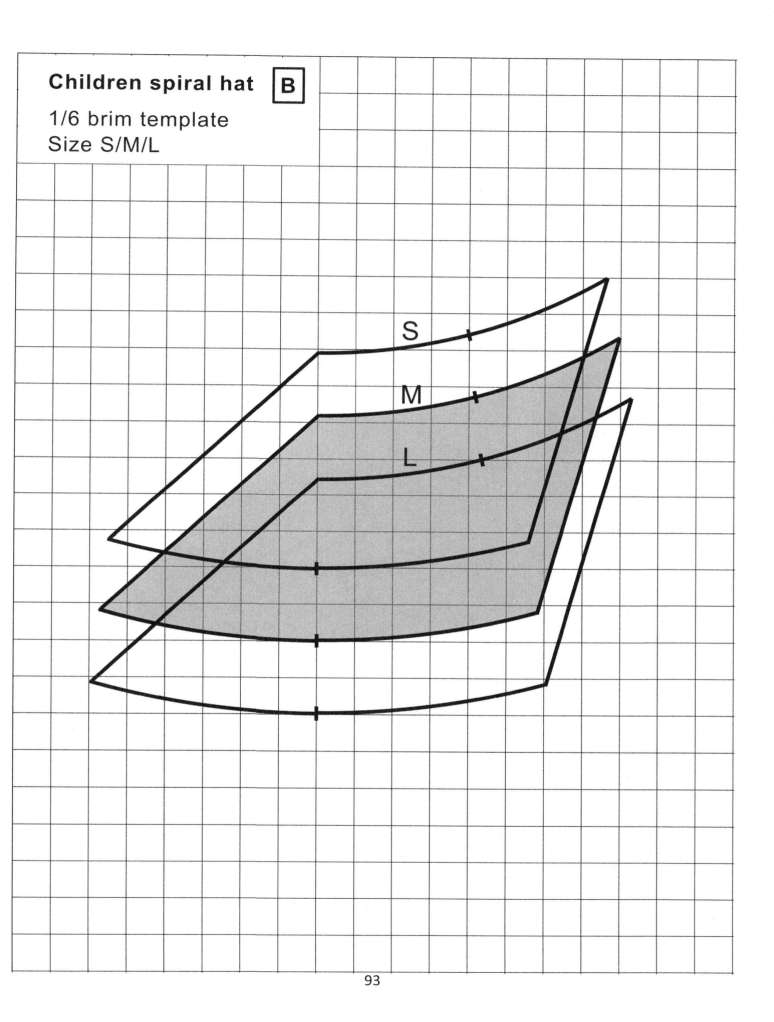

Children spiral hat B

1/6 brim template
Size S/M/L

S

M

L

This page is intentionally blank

Making your own hats

Sewing patterns
by Makapolo Design

ISBN: 979-8461580605

Vol. 1 – Bucket hat sewing patterns

basic pattern size S/M/L for children and adults, and creative patterns size S/M/L for adults

ISBN: 979-8467136004

Vol. 2 – Easy bucket hat sewing patterns

size S/M/L for children and adults, plus band varieties that match the styles

ISBN: 979-8793012485

Vol. 3 – Six and eight panel hat sewing patterns

size S/M/L for children and adults, with volume and brim variations

ISBN: 979-8417324109

Vol. 4 – Creative cut-and-join hat sewing patterns

size S/M/L for children and adults

ISBN: 979-8804645435

Vol. 5 – Patchwork bucket hat sewing patterns

size S/M/L for children and adults

The how-to of

Making your own hats

Step-by-step guide

from basic to creative sewing patterns

Plus practical tips and construction techniques

by Makapolo Design

The foundation laid down in this book, as well as all detailed tips and tricks provided, will assist you in developing your original headdresses with pride and joy. Without the need of any specialized tools, or of being a professional milliner, **anybody with basic sewing skills** can do!

Step-by-step guide

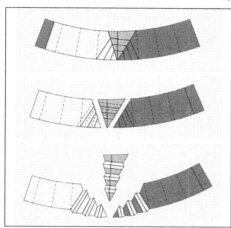

From basic understanding, to the more creative ideas, every step is explained through easy-to-follow illustrations.

Original designs

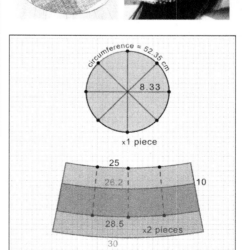

Three basic shapes and seven creative patterns based on my original design, plus four simple embellishment ideas are included.

How-to-construct demo

Detailed construction is demonstrated for one form of six-panel visor cap, with practical tips and tricks from experiences.

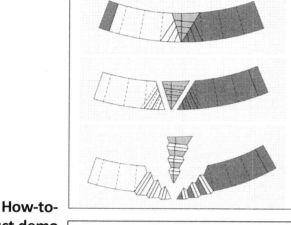

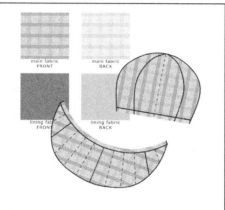

Proven techniques

Simple mathematical techniques, and addition-subtraction method, are proven useful in making the hat sewing patterns.

Available in multiple formats on Amazon; *e-book* (ASIN: B09BBQ7PD6), *black & white interior paperback* (ISBN: 979-8547186349), and *color interior paperback* (ISBN: 979-8547221675)

Stitching Textures

Modern smocking designs and techniques

by MsKapolo Design

Available in two paperback formats on Amazon;
black & white interior
(ISBN: 979-8449727510),
and ***color interior***
(ISBN: 979-8449727466)

Understanding about fancy pleat forming

Learn how to design and create decorative art of smocking in different styles, using a simple square grid, based on few basic knowledges about how fancy textures are formed.

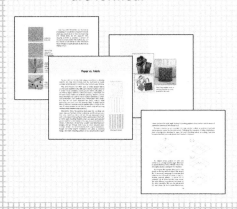

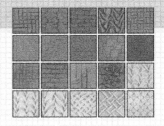

A collection of 32 fascinating patterns

Various hand-smocking patterns from 4 different techniques, as well as paper folding crease diagrams to validate and compare, are collected here in one place.

Systematical approaches

Designs based on the so called "*basic elements*," as well as relations between the starting and finished dimensions, are explained in a systematical manner, allowing a precise calculation for any desired sizing.

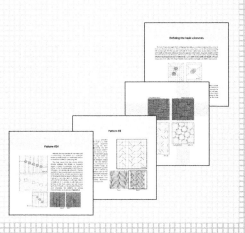

Or, how about triangular grid designs?

ISBN: 979-8809178761

ORIGAMI TESSELLATION STYLE
MODERN SMOCKING PATTERN
Vol. 02

Honeycomb tiling and spreading hexagon
sewing templates for textured berets
and square cushion covers

ISBN: 979-8794174618

ORIGAMI TESSELLATION STYLE
MODERN SMOCKING PATTERN
Vol. 01

Six-fold floral tiling design in two sizes
sewing templates for textured berets
and square cushion covers

More smocking patterns
by MoKapolo Design
are available on Amazon

Beautiful artwork collections for cross-stitching

Cross-stitch patterns by TheCrossStitch by MsKapolo

Available in full colors on Amazon

ISBN: 979-8482453230

ISBN: 979-8778228108

ISBN: 979-8488124752

ISBN: 979-8496077293

ISBN: 979-8769153648

ISBN: 979-8782372408

ISBN: 979-8769786532

ISBN: 979-8490422662

AMAZING GEOMETRIC SHAPES
THE COLORING BOOK

by Makapolo T. S.

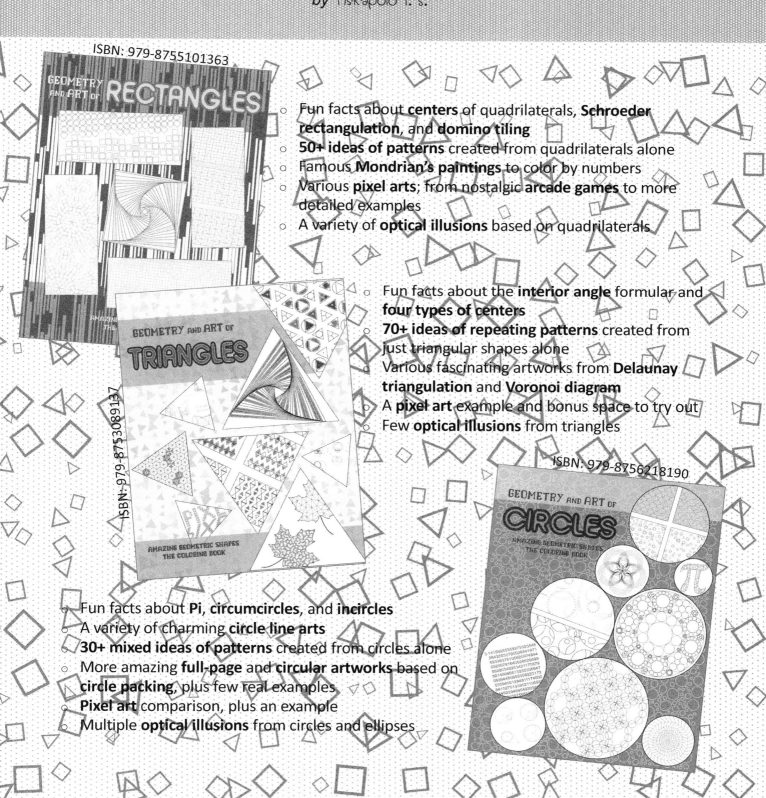

ISBN: 979-8755101363

o Fun facts about **centers** of quadrilaterals, **Schroeder rectangulation**, and **domino tiling**
o **50+ ideas of patterns** created from quadrilaterals alone
o Famous **Mondrian's paintings** to color by numbers
o Various **pixel arts**; from nostalgic **arcade games** to more detailed examples
o A variety of **optical illusions** based on quadrilaterals

o Fun facts about the **interior angle** formular and **four types of centers**
o **70+ ideas of repeating patterns** created from just triangular shapes alone
o Various fascinating artworks from **Delaunay triangulation** and **Voronoi diagram**
o A **pixel art** example and bonus space to try out
o Few **optical illusions** from triangles

ISBN: 979-8753089137

ISBN: 979-8756218190

o Fun facts about **Pi**, **circumcircles**, and **incircles**
o A variety of charming **circle line arts**
o **30+ mixed ideas of patterns** created from circles alone
o More amazing **full-page** and **circular artworks** based on **circle packing**, plus few real examples
o **Pixel art** comparison, plus an example
o Multiple **optical illusions** from circles and ellipses

We create our books with love and care.
But mistakes can always happen. If you find any issues
such as faulty bindings and/or printing errors,
please contact the platform you bought this book from,
and ask for replacement.

And if you enjoy this book, please don't forget to leave
a review on Amazon. Just a simple one will help us a lot.

For further comments or queries regarding the contents
and/or design of this book, please feel free
to email mskapolo.s@gmail.com.

Printed in Great Britain
by Amazon

80768161R00061